SAY YES!

Experience a Life
So Full and Rich
You'll Never Turn Back

RICK RENNER

FOREWORD BY JOYCE MEYER

Harrison House
Tulsa, OK

As I read *Say Yes!* I began to see the mercy of God unfold. Not only does this book talk to you about the call of God on your life, but it traces that call from its inception to its fulfillment. Along the way are the trials and persecutions of Satan that every one of us has to face. God gives you a call despite your past mistakes, and your future mistakes won't remove it. You're going to enjoy this book!

— *Pastor Bob Yandian*
Grace Fellowship Church
Tulsa, Oklahoma

Rick and Denise Renner have an apostolic calling to the people of the former Soviet Union. Their work for God's Kingdom in the Riga and Moscow churches, Russian television, books, and seminars is helping turn the tide for a multitude of people.

Rick writes this book out of his heart. He confronts important issues that must be addressed to release the potential in your life. His personal illustrations let you know he has lived through the truths he is sharing. As you read the book, get ready to hear from the Holy Spirit!

— *Pastor Billy Joe Daugherty*
Victory Christian Center
Tulsa, Oklahoma

In Rick Renner's book *Say Yes!* Rick charges you, challenges you, and encourages you in his inimitable way to *get on the ball, get off the pew, and get out where the fighting is so you can accomplish what God has called you to do*!

This book is written in such a fascinating way, you can't wait to finish one page so you can get to the next page! Every chapter in this awesome book should be devoured slowly and every sentence relished because every word is a gem in itself. *Say Yes!* will be especially challenging and comforting to you if you've never quite stepped out to do what God has called you to do. It will make you take a longer step than you ever have in your whole life!

— *Charles and Frances Hunter*

This book was very well done — easy to read, easy to understand, and easy to apply to everyday life. Rick Renner couldn't have made it more simple to understand that success is doing what God has called you to do. He's also made it very clear how to get *into* God's will if you're *out of* His will. After reading this book, *no one* will have an excuse for failure!

Rick's sharing of all the hardships Paul experienced was also very encouraging to me. Nothing could stop Paul, and nothing should stop us from obeying God either! God certainly uses everyday people — people who are totally dependent on Him. That means we can all make it!

— *Jim Kaseman*
Jim Kaseman Ministries/AFCM
(Association of Faith Ministers
and Churches)

Say Yes!
Experience a Life So Full and Rich
That You'll Never Turn Back

ISBN-13: 978-1-60683-974-4
Copyright © 1999 by Rick Renner
8316 E. 73rd St., Suite 207
Tulsa, OK 74133

Revised Edition 2014
1st Printing

Published by Harrison House Publishers
Tulsa, OK 74145
In partnership with Institute Books, Inc.
Tulsa, OK 74133

Editorial Consultant: Cynthia Hansen
Text Design: Lisa Simpson

DEDICATION

I dedicate this book to a precious friend and partner, *Ann Noel.* God sent you into our lives many years ago at a critical moment in the development of our ministry. You have been a supreme example of the kind of person God is looking to use.

Thank you for your devotion to the Lord, your eagerness to share what He has put in your hands, and your obedience to Him regardless of age, place, or difficulties you have faced in your own walk of faith. Because you are a vessel God can use, millions of lives have been impacted by the Good News of the Gospel. *Denise and I cherish your friendship, and we respect the godly example you have been to us.*

CONTENTS

CHAPTER SEVEN

Exactly What Kind of People

Chapter Ten
What To Do if God Chooses You, But You Feel Like Giving Up

FOREWORD

In 1991, God told Rick Renner to move to the former Soviet Union. It did not make sense to his head; yet his spirit was excited, and he knew wonderful things were in store. Today millions view his television broadcasts, and he is seeing the rewards of obedience.

In *Say Yes!* Rick has clearly established that many are called, but few are chosen. Why is this the case? What are the necessary requirements for not only being called, but chosen as well? What is the cost of fulfilling God's call upon your life? Rick exposes all the requirements necessary to *say yes* to and fulfill your God-given destiny.

Looking at the lives of Paul, David, Saul, and Samuel, Rick exposes all the requirements needed to fulfill your God-given destiny. From lessons learned through his own experiences in ministry, Rick also shares examples of what to do and what to avoid when choosing ministry leaders.

This book details the indispensable qualities needed for leadership. You will be provoked to discipline, encouraged to obedience, and chastised unto righteousness by the unchanging truths shared in this volume.

I highly recommend this book. Rick Renner is an outstanding Bible teacher and my personal friend. I believe your life and ministry will be enriched as you open your heart to him in the following pages.

Joyce Meyer

INTRODUCTION

Throughout the past quarter of a century, I've seen masses of people respond as I've preached, taught, and challenged them to devote their lives to being used by God in some special way. This same thirst to be used by God is evident in the people of the former USSR, where I have lived since 1991.

The result of this spiritual thirst in the former Soviet Union is a move of God so mighty, it can be compared to the divine outpouring that precipitated the events in the book of Acts. The present move of God's Spirit in this region of the world is unprecedented in our generation, and it is one in which I am so thankful God has called me to participate in a significant way.

My point is this: All over the world, people who love God hunger and thirst to be used by Him in some special way. They want their lives to count for His Kingdom. They know they were born to do something significant, but too often they haven't discovered God's plan yet or they don't feel qualified to be used by Him. These believers have questions about how to know God's will; how to know if He's calling them to do this or that; how to be certain they are taking the right steps and are not making a mistake; and how to know whether or not they're really ready to be used by God at this point in their lives.

It is for these hungry-hearted people that I have written this book, *Say yes?* To the best of my ability, I have written what

God has put in my heart for my spiritual "flock" all over the world.

It is my prayer that God will speak to your own heart as you read the following pages. I believe that as I share my personal life experiences and teach vital principles from God's Word, you'll be encouraged to keep going forward until you successfully fulfill God's will for your life. So please carefully study each chapter and meditate on the teachings you are about to read. Each word has been carefully chosen and written with you in mind.

Pursuing the will of God is an adventure. Those who dare to step out into the life of obedience will never feel bored or complain that life is monotonous. The truth is, the life of obedience is the most exciting, challenging, and rewarding experience in this earthly realm!

As you read this book, I trust that you will be encouraged to *step out* in obedience to God's voice; *stay on track* regardless of the obstacles you meet along the way; and *stay open* to the Lord's refining fire so you can be used in the highest and greatest way!

Rick Renner

CHAPTER 1

Is God Pointing His Finger
at You Today?

Just as God spoke to Abraham, telling him to leave his country and follow Him to another land, God also spoke to me several years ago and told me to move my family to the Soviet Union. His message to me was clear: *"Get up, get out of your country, and follow Me to a new home where I have wonderful things in store for you."*

It was the spring of 1991, and the Soviet Union was still fully in force. The Soviet hammer and sickle flew on Union of Soviet Socialist Republic flags throughout the vast space of the Soviet Union's eleven time zones. Lenin still reigned supreme as the god of Soviet atheistic communism. His image loomed over the landscape in the form of monuments, statues, and paintings that could be found in every city, village, factory, and school. His face was even printed on the Russian ruble so that every time someone pulled out money to buy bread, the image of Lenin passed through that person's hands.

At that time, Gorbachev was still in power and the communists were still running the show from deep within the Moscow Kremlin. Soviet troops marched on the streets of every city. The KGB was still carrying out its ruthless orders against Christians, who were considered to be dangerous threats to the existence of the State. In fact, the highest level of KGB espionage was being employed to monitor believers' activities.

On top of all this, the Soviet economy had totally crashed and burned. The government was rationing the most basic products, such as sugar, milk, butter, flour, and meat. Automobiles sat unused in garages because there was no gasoline to purchase. It was an economic mess so terrible that no fiction writer could have ever dreamed up so frightful a scenario.

As I considered all these factors, the idea of moving my family to the USSR seemed *horrifying* to me. What man in his right mind would want to move his family into that kind of predicament? However, I knew God had to have something great in store for our family or He wouldn't want to move us there. My mind reeled at the very thought of obeying what God had put in my heart.

You see, my spirit was willing, but my flesh was weak. My emotions interpreted God's call to the Soviet Union this way: "Leave everything you've worked for; abandon everything you've built; and follow My voice to a country where they hate Christians and where there is no money, nor any visible way to financially support your ministry."

I thought, *At least when God called Abraham, he was called to a beautiful land!* But I was being called to a dilapidated, broken-down land, littered with nuclear debris and environmental toxins. It didn't sound anything like the land of milk and honey that became Abraham's destination! Did God really expect me to leave our growing ministry and beautiful home in Tulsa, Oklahoma, and relocate to a country where everything looked like a ghetto? *Give me a break, Lord!*

After wrangling with God for several months, I threw in the towel and surrendered to His call on our lives. If He wanted us and our ministry in the USSR, then that's where we'd go. I struggled deeply as I thought about all we were losing and leaving behind.

Little did I know what amazing wonders God had in store for our family and ministry. I couldn't have even begun to fathom how miraculously God would use us when He first pointed His finger at me and said, *"Get up, get out of your country, and follow Me to another place where I have wonderful things in store for you."*

I did know, however, that if I didn't tell anyone what God had told me, no one except God and me would know if I disobeyed that divine mandate. My flesh was tempted to do just that. It wanted to say, "No, thank You, Lord. I'm staying right here in good ol' Tulsa, Oklahoma, where I'm enjoying the sweet taste of success, along with all my faith buddies!"

A DAYDREAM OR A VISION FROM HEAVEN?

When I look at what God has done in our lives and ministry since that infamous move in 1991, I am reminded of an experience I had with Him when I was an 18-year-old boy. What God told me during that experience was so huge and fantastic, I wondered at the time, *Could this really be God speaking to me? Could He really use me in such a big way? Is this really the voice of God — or just a daydream?*

This spiritual experience occurred during college spring break while I was visiting my missionary cousins in Mexico City. One evening as I attended a church in the outskirts of the city, the Holy Spirit began to speak to my heart, giving me concrete facts about my life and future. (The Bible tells us in Isaiah 46:10 and John 16:13 that God knows the end from the beginning and will show us things to come.) The Holy Spirit's words were so vivid that I reached for a piece of paper to write down what He was communicating to my spirit.

That night God pulled opened the curtains of the spirit realm and allowed me to see a sneak preview of my future ministry. It took me off guard. This vision of future ministry seemed too grand for a boy my age. Yet the words I was hearing seemed so loud in my heart that I wondered if anyone else could hear them as well.

Before this experience, I'd known God's call was on my life, but I'd never had a distinct vision of *how* God would use me. But that night the Holy Spirit communicated crystal-clear details to me about my divine call.

I kept writing. If this was really God's voice speaking to me, *He was calling me to be a spokesman to the nations.* I even heard Him say that my voice would be carried across the sky to the nations of the earth via the airwaves. *What did He mean by airwaves?*

I wondered if my mind was playing tricks. Was this just a daydream? I folded my piece of paper, inserted it into my Bible, and stored it away in a secret place where no one would find it. I was apprehensive that if anyone ever read what I'd written, they'd laugh at me and dismiss my experience as a childish dream.

As loudly and clearly as I'd heard the message, it still seemed too grandiose for a boy from Sand Springs, Oklahoma. Years later, however, I remembered this experience and realized it *was* God's voice I had heard speaking to me that night.

That was nearly three decades ago. As I write this book, our television program "Good News With Rick Renner" has a potential viewing audience of more than 110 million people each week. The Lord has given us the goal to keep expanding until we reach *one billion* potential weekly viewers! What God told me that night in Mexico City when I was 18 years old is *exactly* what has come to pass in my life.

A few years ago, I came across that little container I used as a teenager to hide my treasured possessions. As I sifted through the information contained there, I found the original little piece of paper from Mexico City. Scribbled in my teenaged hand-writing was the "word" God had given me about being a spokesman to the nations. *God had planted His dream in my heart, even at that early age.*

Although for a long time I'd assumed that my experience in that Mexican church was just the result of a young teenager's imagination, this word from the Lord *precisely* described His call on my life. Certainly it wasn't something this boy would have ever dreamed up or thought of by himself!

WHAT ARE YOUR DREAMS?

Has God put a dream in your heart? Has He told you to do something that is so huge, you're tempted to dismiss it as silly nonsense? Do you ask yourself, *Is this idea really from God or just a case of crazy daydreaming?*

Be careful not to dismiss your dream too quickly! It may be a vision of your future that God has dropped down inside your spirit. When these God-given dreams occasionally surface in your mind, you may misinterpret them as "wishful thinking" or "fantasies." But have you considered the possibility that God may be trying to break into your conscious mind to reveal His plan to you?

> Be careful not to dismiss your dream too quickly! It may be a vision of your future that God has dropped down inside your spirit.

As a child of God, you have incredible potential. The Spirit who raised Jesus from the dead resides inside you (Romans 8:11). He wants to unlock His divine power and flood you with supernatural power to make things happen in your life. *He's just waiting for you to believe!*

If you sense that God is pointing His finger at you right now, I can relate to where you are and to what you're feeling. I've sensed my Heavenly Father's finger pointed at *me* on many occasions — poking me in the ribs, wagging in my face, or nudging me from behind as He tells me to get with the program and make a decision or get out of the way so someone else can take my place.

Hesitation is fine for a while, especially if you're taking the time to confirm you're on the right track. But when hesitation is prolonged again and again, it's usually a subtle form of rebellion. Your flesh doesn't want to do what God has told you to do. It doesn't feel comfortable or secure because it doesn't know how to accomplish the assigned task. Therefore, the flesh likes to look for excuses to put off obedience just a little longer.

If you don't finally say, "Yes, Lord, I'll do what You say and go where You tell me to go," the Lord will find someone else to do the job. He won't sit around and wait on you forever. There comes a deciding moment when you must get with it or get out of the way so someone else can get started.

Don't forget that the Lord Jesus taught, "For many are called, but few are chosen" (Matthew 22:14). There are "many" who have had opportunity to do something great and significant, but because they wouldn't go on with God, they were not "chosen" to do it. *Don't let that be you!*

THERE'S NO MORE TIME FOR EXCUSES!

When I first started walking with God, I was anxious about taking a step of faith. I wanted to do everything God told me to do, but because this faith walk was new to me, I didn't feel confident. As I began to step out to obey God's instructions, I'd wonder, *Can I do this? Am I doing it the way I'm supposed to do it? Am I sure God is telling me to do this, or is it all just my imagination?* I fretted like this quite a bit, afraid of making a mistake and looking like a fool.

For instance, I remember the first time the Holy Spirit moved on me to give a prophetic word in a church service. The worship service fell silent, and everyone waited for the prophetic word to come forth. I knew I was the one who had the "word." My heart pounded wildly in my chest as each silent moment passed.

I told myself, *If no one else gives it within the next minute, then I'll prophesy.* I looked at my watch and waited. I desperately hoped someone else would start prophesying and alleviate the heavy burden I felt, but no one else gave the prophetic word. I prayed silently, *Just a few more minutes, Lord. If no one else gives the word, then I'll give it.*

Five minutes passed. My heart was beating harder and harder. Beads of perspiration trickled down my brow. I knew if I didn't give the word of prophecy, I would be *disobedient.* Finally, with great trepidation I opened my mouth and began to speak the prophetic word to the congregation.

I finally brought my flesh into agreement with my spirit so I could prophesy, but it didn't happen instantly. It took a little time to deal with my flesh and work up the nerve to open my mouth and say, *"Thus saith the Lord…"*

Over the years, I've found myself facing that same tendency to hesitate again and again. But years of experience have taught me that if I will do exactly what God tells me, His power makes up for all the insufficiencies and weaknesses I feel.

> Years of experience have taught me that if I will do exactly what God tells me, His power makes up for all the insufficiencies and weaknesses I feel.

You see, *when we feel weak is actually when God's power shows up the strongest* (2 Corinthians 12:9,10).

But before I learned that lesson, I made the mistake for many years of asking a lot of "what if" questions — questions like "What if I fail?" or "What if it doesn't work as I expected?" Questions like these often put the brakes on our walk with the Lord, hindering us from accepting and conquering glorious new assignments God wants to entrust to us.

Too many believers present God with a host of arguments as to why He should choose someone else. They lay their ill-conceived case before God as a lawyer would present his defense before a judge and jury:

- "I can't speak well enough."

- "I see that other people are more talented."

- "I don't think I'm ready yet."

- "I'm afraid."

- "I don't know how I'll be able to pay for it."

- "I'm too fat."

- "I'm too skinny."

- "I'm not handsome enough."

- "I'm not popular enough."

- "I don't have enough time to do it."

- "I'm not the best choice."

Some people don't even try to come up with an excuse. They just tell the Lord:

- "It's not in my heart to do what You're asking."

- "I just don't want to do it!"

- "NO! I won't do it!"

You can argue with God all day long about why He should choose someone besides you. But until you quit fighting and simply surrender your will to obey God, you will never lay hold of your divine purpose in life.

> Until you quit fighting and simply surrender your will to obey God, you will never lay hold of your divine purpose in life.

God has a specific calling for *you*. The spiritual race He has set before you is one that no one else can run. And when you finally step out to obey Him, you'll be so glad you did! There is no greater satisfaction or peace than in knowing you are doing exactly what God has called you to do.

Your flesh may recoil from doing what God has asked because flesh likes to stay in its comfort zone where it isn't necessary to change, grow, and develop. But as a child of God, you can take charge of your flesh! Tell it to stop its ranting and raving. For too long your flesh has told you all the lame reasons why you can't be used by God. It's time for your flesh to stop controlling your destiny!

> **It's time for your flesh to stop controlling your destiny!**

If you don't step out in faith to do what you *know* you're supposed to do, you'll miss the whole reason God brought you into this world. You see, He didn't bring you into the world just to take up space on planet earth. He has something grand and glorious for you to do. And if you miss that plan, you will answer for it when you stand before the Judgment Seat of Christ (2 Corinthians 5:10).

Imagine what a horrible tragedy it would be for you to live out your entire life, only to discover when you die that you missed the grand, glorious destiny God had planned for you. God forbid the thought of it! Rather than go on living a ho-hum, monotonous, humdrum life that gives you no happiness or joy, turn your faith loose! Jump out into the river of God, and let it carry you to a vast ocean of supernatural experiences and conquests. *That's God's idea of a great life!*

DOES YOUR LIFE HAVE A PURPOSE?

Let me tell you about an experience I had several years ago when I still lived in Latvia that made a great impact on me. I was invited to hold a series of meetings for three days in the nearby Russian city of Pskov. Instead of spending hours flying on a plane to Moscow and then catching another plane to Pskov, my associate and I decided to drive the distance from Riga to Pskov. We looked forward to seeing the countryside along the way.

After four hours of driving, we finally arrived at the Latvian border, where we expected to cross over into Russia. To our surprise, travelers were not allowed to use this particular border crossing, so the border guard directed us to another crossing about thirty kilometers away. However, in order to get there, we had to drive the bumpiest, most difficult roads I've ever encountered anywhere in the world. That thirty kilometers took hours!

But when we finally reached our destination, we were told we couldn't cross over into Russia there either! The border guards directed us to a third border crossing. After another four grueling hours of driving, we finally reached a border that had a Custom's Post, where we were allowed to pass from Latvia into Russia.

As my associate and I drove along the Latvian/Russia border that afternoon, we were shocked by what we saw. At that time we lived in Riga, the capital of Latvia, a city that was recovering from years of Soviet occupation and was actually starting to bloom and prosper. But as we drove along the Latvian border that afternoon, I was taken back in my memories to those hard times in 1991 when the Soviet people had no hope.

The towns we passed looked like they were dying. People wore black and gray clothing. The buildings looked gray. The clouds looked oppressive. Every face we passed along the street seemed to wear a blank stare. Even the mildest form of a facial expression was rare. Young men not even 20 years old stumbled down the streets all day long — mornings, afternoons, and evenings — under the influence of vodka.

Because of the economic woes that had hit those small towns, every factory we passed was closed. Windows were broken out. Parking lots were piled high with old, rusted junk. It was an ecological nightmare. Entire villages were unemployed. Tall, Soviet-style apartments were filled with tenants who had no jobs and no income — not even enough money to buy bread to feed their families or to purchase clothes for their children.

Highly educated people now scurried here and there to peddle goods from their homes, trying to scrape a little money together so they could buy enough food to keep themselves and their families alive. These people had no work, no purpose, no reason to even get up in the morning. It was "survival of the fittest" in the truest sense of the word.

Desperation is the word that kept coming to my mind as we passed through these border villages. *The people we drove past that day had lost every reason for living.* When the great, mighty Soviet dream had collapsed and died, it had left them with no foundation, no goal or sense of direction, no purpose, no identity.

With this gaping vacancy in their souls and no jobs in sight to provide some glimmer of hope, many of the people turned to the bottle to drown their overwhelming misery. It was a Soviet wasteland, a nightmare more horrible than the screenwriter of a disaster movie could ever conceive in his wildest imaginations.

I kept thinking, *If I lived here without God, I'd have lost my reason for living too. Without the hope of Jesus Christ, I might have even turned to the bottle to drown my miseries, just as many of these people have.*

These precious people hadn't turned to alcohol with the goal of becoming alcoholics. It was just the only way they knew how to cope with the disaster they were experiencing in their lives. I felt such emotion wash over me as my heart broke for these downhearted souls. When I looked in their faces, I saw what they were feeling:

- Hopelessness

- Purposelessness

- Desperation

- Downheartedness

- Pointlessness

- Feelings of Abandonment

- Feelings of Being Discarded

- Heartache

It shook me as we passed by each village. I cried inside for these people whom God had created to be something special in this world. Yet the uniqueness, the special individuality that God created each one of them to express, had been lost in a sea of disappointment.

> People live and die without ever really knowing the reason for their existence — why they were born and what they're supposed to do with their lives.

I have an apostolic call to the people of the former USSR. This is why my heart especially beats and bleeds for them and their spiritual condition. But this problem of purposelessness is not unique to the nations of the former Soviet Union.

All over the world, people live with no sense of direction. They live and die without ever really knowing the reason for their existence — why they were born and what they're supposed to do with their lives. This is true of people in every nation, city, and village in the world. It is even true of believers when they don't understand how to discover and follow God's plan for their lives.

Of the millions of letters I receive from television viewers around the world, the number-one category of questions people ask reflects this widespread sense of purposelessness. They ask:

- "What am I supposed to be doing with my life?"

- "How can I know God's will?"

- "Does God really want to use me?"

- "Am I fit to be used by God in some special way?"

It doesn't matter what their country of origin is, what language they speak, or from what financial and political background they've come, human beings want to know why they were placed on this earth. They want to know what God wants them to do and how to get started doing it.

If a man has no revelation of why he was born or what God has called him to do, his quality of life is reduced to a very low level. Even though all the possibilities of the human spirit reside within him, he will never enjoy the great potential locked up inside him until he has a revelation of his divine purpose on this earth.

A PURPOSE FOR EVERYTHING UNDER THE HEAVENS

Human beings are not the only species in God's creation that are born with a purpose to fulfill. Everything God has ever made was created with a specific design and function in mind.

> Everything God has ever made was created with a specific design and function in mind.

For instance, several years ago, the wolf population was growing too fast in Yellowstone National Park, Wyoming. The governmental agency in charge decided that the rapid population growth of these wolves had to be stopped. To solve the problem, wolves were captured and transported to other parts of the nation. Some wolves were shot and killed.

Soon the wolf population was greatly reduced. People sang the praises of this wolf management program. The move to regulate the numbers of wolves in Yellowstone Park was hailed a "success."

But after a few years, the deer population grew to be so enormous that it became a danger to vehicles and drivers. Deer even roamed the streets and sidewalks of Yellowstone Park. They also infiltrated the nearby local farmlands, where they trampled and ate the farmers' crops. They even wandered into people's yards. Deer were everywhere!

Suddenly, everyone began to verbally assault the governmental agency responsible for killing or transferring most of the Yellowstone wolves. If the agency hadn't transported or killed so many wolves, the deer population would never have gotten so out of hand.

Without the wolves, the balance of nature had gotten out of order. In the end, governmental officials decided that wolves had to be brought back to Yellowstone in order to restore balance to the animal kingdom of that region.

The point I'm making is that even wolves have a very important *purpose.* Ecclesiastes 3:1 says, "To every thing there is a season, and a time to every purpose under the heaven." Everything has a purpose, or it wouldn't be here on this earth.

When you study the animal and plant life on planet earth, it quickly becomes obvious that God made everything with a purpose. In fact, although it may sound ludicrous, even mice, snakes, and insects have a purpose in nature that's very important. Remove them, and the whole ecological system would go out of balance.

Trees and plants also have a strategic part in the earth's eco-system. Those green leaves are God's filtration system to cleanse the air so we won't suffocate to death! *Yes, even leaves have a purpose!*

Seas, lakes, rivers, and creeks have a purpose as well. They carry vital water and nutrients that nourish the earth. When rivers overflow and flood, we look at it as a tragedy. But even those overflowing waters have an important purpose. They carry fresh, precious minerals that renourish the land so it can keep producing crops.

The clouds in the sky overhead also have a very important purpose. They store moisture that later descends as rain upon the earth. They also block out dangerous ultraviolet rays of sunlight that would damage our sensitive human skin and burn up all the earth's vegetation. Clouds are not just pretty puffs of white to decorate the sky. *They have a purpose!*

You Are 'Under Heaven' — So You Have a Special Purpose!

Everything God made was created with a special design and function. If this is true of the animal and plant kingdoms, then how much more true is it that *you* have a special purpose in this world? You were not born simply to occupy space — to eat food, go to the bathroom, sleep, and get up the next morning to start the same dull, boring routine all over again. *No!* There is a reason you are here on this earth. You have a God-assigned, God-given purpose.

> **You were not born simply to occupy space!**

Remember, Ecclesiastes 3:1 says, "To *every thing* there is a season, and a time to every purpose under the heaven." According to this verse, if you are *"under the heaven,"* then you have a *"purpose"*! You are not here by accident! There is a great Designer who planned every detail of who you are and the glorious plan you are to fulfill!

When a person never locks into his God-given purpose or assignment in life, he wanders aimlessly from one thing to the next. This is the reason *unbelievers* drink, use drugs, and frequently go from one relationship to another. They are trying to fill that hole they feel deep inside.

This is also why *believers* aren't satisfied with their marriages and constantly trade jobs. *They are seeking to fill a hole that can only be filled by knowing they are doing what God wants them to do.*

Money cannot fill that hole. Relationships cannot fill that hole. Jobs cannot fill that hole. *That hole is only filled when you step into God's will and have the satisfaction of knowing you're right smack dab in the middle of His plan for your life.*

I guarantee you that if you're trying to fill that hole with your marriage, you will be constantly dissatisfied with that relationship. If you're trying to fill that hole with money, your riches will never satisfy you, no matter how much money you accumulate.

> **Are you doing what God wants you to do? You won't be happy doing anything else.**

In fact, if you are struggling in any area of your life — your identity, your job, your marriage, or your finances — and it seems that nothing ever satisfies you, perhaps you need to ask a deeper question. *Are you doing what God wants you to do?* You won't be happy doing anything else.

You Need a Vision for Your Life

You need a God-given vision for your life. Without it, you'll always wander and flounder. Proverbs 29:18 says, "Where there is no vision, the people perish: but he that keepeth the law, happy is he."

What I saw on the Latvian/Russian border that day was a picture of what happens when people exist with no vision or sense of direction for their lives. When there is no clear-cut direction or goal for which to live, human beings feel *purposeless.* When that hopeless feeling seizes the heart, mind, and emotions, it doesn't take long until man begins to slide into a pit of despair. It's just as the Bible says: *"Where there is no vision, the people perish...."*

What does the Bible mean when it says people "perish" if they have no vision? Several good translations of Proverbs 29:18 are as follows:

- "Where there is no vision, the people live purposeless, meaningless lives...."

- "Where there is no vision, the people have no sense of direction and lose their reason for living...."

- "Where there is no vision, people become lazy, dissatisfied, and sluggish...."

- "Where there is no vision, the people cast off restraint and become undisciplined and unproductive...."

People need a sense of direction. They need borders. They need guidelines.

And that includes me as well! I can personally testify that when I have no purpose, vision, or goal for my life, I sink to unbelievably low levels of inactivity and laziness. It's just a fact of life that I need something to shoot for and to keep me going.

God put it into the heart of man to take dominion (Genesis 1:26) and to achieve something great with his life. When man loses that purpose — that God-birthed spark in his heart to reach out for something great and significant — he becomes dysfunctional, lazy, lethargic, languid, and lackadaisical in his approach to life. That's why a person needs a challenging goal to aim for with his life.

When that person has a vision before him, he has a goal to live for and an objective for which to shoot. This gives meaning to his existence, a purpose and plan designed specifically for his life. It gives him a reason to get up in the morning, a reason to keep fighting against the odds he encounters along the way. A vision gives him inspiration and motivation to keep striving until he's reached what God put in his heart.

Maintaining a clear-cut, unambiguous, indisputable vision is vital for my life. It is like a trail I can follow. That trail may occasionally lead me through dense forests, dry places, and even occasional danger. But I know that if I stay on track, the vision God placed in my heart will lead me to His destination for my life.

> **I know that if I stay on track, the vision God placed in my heart will lead me to His destination for my life.**

If I get off track and try to take another route, it always gets me in trouble. The vision God gave me is like a rock I can lay hold of and hang on to. It is like a beacon that keeps me on track with my faith, my marriage, my family, my church, my ministry, my time, my energy, my money, and my efforts.

- When I have a vision, I live a full, meaningful, and rewarding life.

- When I have a vision, I live with a sense of direction and experience a reason for living.

- When I have a vision, I am disciplined, diligent, hard-working, and full of energy.

- When I have a vision, I feel fruitful, productive, and satisfied with my life.

WHAT IS A VISION?

But let's step back for a moment and ask, *"What is a vision?"* The word "vision" in Hebrew means *to see*. It is the idea of having a mental image so sharp and so clear that you are able to "picture" something in your mind. This is not an abstract idea you can't latch on to; it's a concept so concrete that you can easily grab hold of it and say, *"That's it! I see it! I know exactly what I'm supposed to be doing with my life."*

When God first called me to inundate the former Soviet Union with His Word by broadcasting it on television into as many homes and regions as possible, such a thought was the farthest thing from my imagination. It had never before even entered my mind!

But when God spoke to me, I was able to "see" what He was asking me to do. It wasn't just an abstruse, fanciful notion floating somewhere out in the spirit realm. It was a dream that took shape and materialized in my heart and mind. I could literally "see" it in my mind. I could visualize precisely what God was calling me to do. It was direction so strong that I could stand on it and move with confidence as I began to fulfill it.

When I think of how God likes to plant His dreams and visions in our hearts, I am reminded of how He spoke to Abraham in Genesis 15. God drew Abraham's attention upward to the stars. And as Abraham visualized the countless stars in the sky overhead, God told him, "...So shall thy seed be" (v. 5).

God put an "image" in Abraham's mind he would never forget. Abraham saw a "vision" of what God wanted to do through him. That vision stayed with Abraham for the rest of his life. He was never able to forget or get away from what he had "pictured" that night when God first spoke to him. That vision is what kept him going year after year, through thick and thin, through good times and bad, until it was finally fulfilled in his life.

It is also important to point out that the Hebrew for "vision" is the same identical Hebrew word used for "provision." This is fantastic! *This means a vision gives provision!*

> With your vision before you, you have something to pursue, to follow after, to shoot for with your life.

Without a vision, you have no sense of purpose for your existence. But when you have a vision for your life, it provides you with a goal. It gives you purpose, direction, boundaries, limitations, and perimeters. With that vision before you, you have something to pursue, to follow after, to shoot for with your life.

For instance, even when I was a young college kid, I knew God had called me to the ministry. I even knew what kind of ministry I would have. So with that vision before me, I began to pick and choose which classes I needed and did not need.

Because God called me to be an exegetical teacher, I knew I needed to learn ancient Greek and thus enrolled in ancient Greek class. He also informed me that I would be writing books, so I knew I needed to enroll in journalism. My God-given vision provided direction and guidance for my life.

You see, when you know God's will, it simplifies the choices you make in life. God's plan is like a measuring stick to help you measure what is needed or right for your life versus what is *not* needed or *not* right for you.

Right now I have a very specific call to the nations of the former Soviet Union and Europe. Yet every day I am presented with marvelous opportunities to do good things in other parts of the world. But just because they are good things doesn't mean I am the one who's supposed to do them.

I must judge each opportunity by asking myself, *How does this fit into the vision God has given me? Does it fit into the role God has assigned for my life?* If the answer is "This is a great idea, but it doesn't add to the vision God gave me," then I know the opportunity isn't for me. It may be a God-inspired dream for someone to pursue, but I am not that someone.

You see, my vision gives me guidelines and parameters for my life and ministry. Without those parameters, I would run all over the world and end up doing all kinds of good works. I would spend loads of money, expend huge amounts of energy, and invest a lot of valuable time doing *good things* that were not necessarily *right things* for me.

That's why having a vision helps me make the right decisions when faced with these types of choices. It also helps me prioritize when I plan my calendar or when I must choose how to invest my money, time, and energy. I ask myself, *How does this new opportunity fit into the picture God gave me? Does this expenditure promote the vision God gave me to fulfill? Is this the best use of my time and energy, or is this a distraction to pull me away from my God-given assignment?*

FIND AND FULFILL YOUR LIFE ASSIGNMENT

One thing is for sure — when you are assured that God has called you, you should strive to "make your calling and election sure" (2 Peter 1:10). You need to clarify what He has called you to do, cut out all the slack in your life, and go for it with all your heart. You *can* accomplish what God has put in your heart and mind to do, but it's going to take a 100% commitment. Anything less will not do the job.

> You *can* accomplish what God has put in your heart and mind to do, but it's going to take a 100% commitment. Anything less will not do the job.

Do you want to fulfill the task God has especially prepared for you? Do you want the satisfaction of knowing you are doing exactly what you were brought into this world to do? Are you willing to put out the faith necessary to accomplish the job?

When you reach the end of your life, the measure of your success in life will all be wrapped up in one question: *Did you do what God called you to do?* When God spoke to you, did you stay in faith? Did you stubbornly refuse to relinquish that dream because you emphatically knew it was your life assignment?

> When you reach the end of your life, the measure of your success in life will all be wrapped up in one question: *Did you do what God called you to do?*

You may say, "But, Rick, I don't know if God has called me to do anything special!"

> **I must judge each opportunity by asking myself,** *How does this fit into the vision God has given me?*

Of course He did! Do you think He brought you into the world to simply take up space on the planet? Do you think that's all there is for you in this life? If that were the case, you wouldn't be that much different than an animal, would you? Don't animals function on just such a low level of existence, just getting along day by day? Do you actually think God's plans for you would be that low?

God certainly has a call on your life. He has a mission just for you. You may not know it yet, but there is a definite, distinct call of God designed just for your life and for no one else. Ephesians 2:10 says God was choosing, predestining, and planning the very works you should walk in even before the first layer of the earth's crust was laid!

Your presence on this planet was not accidental, nor was it an afterthought. God planned your life. He brought you into this world so you would contribute something valuable.

So seek God diligently until you receive revelation regarding His plan for you. Once that plan is revealed, get into the flow of faith and stay there for the rest of your life. The only way you'll accomplish God's plan is by living in the realm of faith and staying determined to do whatever God asks you to do. Both faith and diligence are required if you want to be successful in fulfilling your God-given life assignment.

QUESTIONS FOR PERSONAL GROWTH OR GROUP DISCUSSION

1. Can you think of a specific dream that God has placed in your heart? Have you been tempted to dismiss that dream because it seemed too huge to fulfill?

2. What will be the consequences if you continue to hesitate and put off obeying God's call to fulfill what He has asked you to do?

3. What is the danger of asking a lot of "What if?" questions when the Lord gives you an assignment?

4. How can you determine whether your hesitancy to take a new direction in your life is the Holy Spirit's "caution signal" in your spirit or your own fearful flesh?

5. What kind of fruit is produced in a person's life when he has no sense of purpose or direction?

Notes:

_____

_____

_____

_____

_____

_____

_____

_____

_____

_____

_____

_____

_____

_____

_____

_____

_____

_____

_____

_____

_____

_____

_____

CHAPTER 2

If God Really Chose You, Why Are You Experiencing So Many Hassles Along the Way?

The devil has never been thrilled about people who dare to do the will of God. Satan knows they have the power to drive darkness away and replace it with the glorious light of the Gospel.

The devil detests that light so much that he tries to put it out before it opens spiritually blind eyes and sets the prisoners free. *To get rid of the light, he often attacks the light-bearer.* You see, Satan knows that if he can discredit, confuse, oppress, or throw the light-bearer off track, he can continue holding tightly to his claims on nations, cities, homes, and people.

If God has called you to do something special, you are a Heaven-sent light-bearer. What you have been asked to do has the power to drive away darkness and bring life-changing truth to people in your environment. To keep you from accomplishing your God-given task, the devil may try to hinder

> To keep you from accomplishing your God-given task, the devil may try to hinder you or even knock you out of the race. That may be one reason you're experiencing so many hassles along the way.

you or even knock you out of the race. That may be one reason you're experiencing so many hassles along the way.

I'm not trying to be pessimistic — just realistic. I want to help you understand the kind of opposition you may face when you start your faith journey. I don't want you to be shocked if the devil tries to resist you along the way.

I know of no great Christian leader who hasn't faced some kind of opposition as he or she sought to do God's will. But the truth is, believers can overcome every attack if they won't quit first!

According to John 1:5, darkness does not have the power to overcome light: "And the light shineth in darkness; and the darkness comprehended it not." The word "comprehended" is the Greek word *katalambano*. It is a compound of the words *kata* and *lambano*.

The word *kata* carries the force of something that is *dominating* or *subjugating*. The word *lambano* means *to seize or grab hold of*. When the two words are compounded, the new word means *to seize, to pull down, to tackle, to conquer,* or *to hold under one's power*. Therefore, this verse could be translated, *"Darkness does not have the ability to suppress or to hold the light under its domain."*

This doesn't mean that darkness won't *attempt* to overcome the light. However, its efforts will be frustrated and unsuccessful because the light of God always prevails, even in what seems to be the darkest hour or the bleakest situation. Darkness simply doesn't have the power or ability to put out God's light. Since you are a child of the light (Ephesians 5:8), this means darkness doesn't have the ability to put out *your* light either!

First John 5:4 says, "For whatsoever is born of God overcometh the world: and this is the victory that overcometh the world, even our faith." The word "overcometh" is the Greek word *nikos*. It means *to conquer.* It was used to portray athletes who had gained the mastery of the competition and ultimately reigned supreme as champions over the games.

> The light of God always prevails, even in what seems to be the darkest hour or the bleakest situation.

The Holy Spirit was careful in His selection of this word *nikos.* This word communicates vivid images that pertain to our walk of faith and victory. First, it tells us that when we begin the walk of faith, we enter into a real-life competition. The decision to walk by faith puts us right smack dab in the center of the ring where the contest immediately begins.

This is so important to understand. You may have supposed that the walk of faith would remove you from problems. But the truth is, your faith pits you directly opposite the devil's powers. Satan may try to go for a knock-out punch. But even if he knocks you flat, he can't keep you down there!

The apostle Paul said he was "...cast down, but not destroyed" (2 Corinthians 4:9). One translation says, *"We occasionally get knocked down, but never get knocked out!"* Those who are born of God have the supernatural ability to keep getting up again, no matter how many times they fall!

The word *nikos* also tells us that we are the ultimate champions. This concept makes me think of Romans 8:37: "Nay, in all these things we are more than conquerors through him that loved us."

> **Those who are born of God have the supernatural ability to keep getting up again, no matter how many times they fall!**

The phrase "more than conquerors" is from the Greek word *hupernikos*, a compound of the word *huper* and this same Greek word, *nikos.* By joining the words *huper* and *nikos* together into one word, Paul makes one fabulous, jam-packed, power-filled statement about you and me!

I quote from Chapter Five of my book, *Dressed To Kill:*

> The phrase "more than" (*huper*) literally means *over, above, and beyond.* It depicts something that is *way beyond measure.* We derive the word "super" from the word *huper.* As used in this passage, it conveys the idea of *superiority.* It means *greater; superior; higher; better; more than a match for; utmost; paramount;* or *foremost.* It also means *to be first-rate, first-class, top-notch, unsurpassed, unequaled, and unrivaled by any person or thing!*

Now Paul uses this word to denote what kind of conquerors we are in Jesus Christ. We are *huper-conquerors*! The word *huper* dramatizes our victory. It means that *we are greater conquerors, superior conquerors, higher and better conquerors. We are more than a match for any adversary or foe. We are utmost conquerors, paramount conquerors, foremost conquerors, first-rate conquerors, first-class conquerors, top-notch conquerors, unsurpassed conquerors, unequaled and unrivaled conquerors!* All of this is what the phrase "more than" means!

The word "conqueror" is from the word *nikos*. It describes *an overcomer, a conqueror, a champion, a victor*, or *a master*. It is the picture of *an overwhelming, prevailing force.* The word *nikos* is a dramatic word that depicts *one who is altogether victorious*! However, *nikos* alone wasn't strong enough to make Paul's point, so he joined the words *huper* and *nikos* together to make his point even stronger!

By calling us "more than conquerors," Paul tells us that in Christ Jesus, we are *overwhelming conquerors, victors paramount*, or *enormous overcomers.* This word is so power-packed that one could translate it "a phenomenal, walloping conquering force"!

So in First John 5:4, the apostle John uses the word *nikos* to describe our superior position as children of God over the world. We are fully armed with everything we need to be super-conquerors in this life. He continues to tell us specifically that we have a "victory that overcometh the world."

You need to especially pay careful attention to the "world" in this verse, since this pertains to our authority over *anything* Satan ever attempts to throw at us. The word "world" is the Greek word *kosmos*. This Greek word always refers to an *ordered system* of such things as society, culture, nature, and even science. Today scientists use the word *kosmos* to describe *the universe*. Although far-flung and ever-expanding, the universe is a system filled with impeccable order.

So when John writes that we have a "victory that overcometh the world," he is actually saying, *"We have a victory that overcomes, masters, and champions itself even over the order of things found in the world."*

Again, this includes *anything* that is "ordered." It would include *politics*, which is an ordered system of governance within a given society. It would include *science*, which is an ordered, systemized study of the physical world. It would also include *economics, culture,* or any other earthly *ordered system*.

In Second Corinthians 4:4, the apostle Paul calls Satan "the god of this world." Here, the word "world" is the Greek word *aiona*. It refers to *all the thoughts, opinions, maxims, speculations, hopes, impulses, and aspirations of a specific generation*. So whereas the word *kosmos* describes an ordered system, the word *aiona* describes the exact thinking of that system. By calling Satan the "god of this world," Paul is telling us that Satan primarily exerts his influence through *world systems*.

For instance, Satan expresses himself through the educational system when it takes an aggressive stand against the principles of God's Word. He also attempts to manipulate the thinking of a lost world with the anti-Christian bias that exists in Hollywood today. This is exactly why believers are depicted as idiots in motion pictures. It's the devil working through a godless entertainment system to poison society against the Church. Finally, Satan also works through world systems of governments to oppose the Gospel and to imprison believers.

Just as God works through Christians and His Church, Satan works through unbelievers and world systems that are not rooted in God's Word. The devil is such a master at working in this worldly sphere that Paul calls him "the god of this world." This world's systems and way of thinking are the primary vehicles through which Satan works.

Why is this so important? Because you need to know that Satan will try to use the world around you to oppose what you are called to do.

For example, when Satan attempts to attack our television ministry in the former Soviet Union, it isn't an invisible, untouchable, unidentifiable attack. Recurrently these attacks come through the government or through a religious organization in which Satan has found a foothold.

> Satan will try to use the world around you to oppose what you are called to do.

He attempts to stop the broadcast of God's Word to multiple millions of spiritually needy people by attacking our cash flow.

Satan doesn't hide in the closet and pop out at night to personally attack us while we're sleeping! He uses people, events, situations, circumstances, and difficult dilemmas to obstruct us from reaching our goals. As the "god of this world," he uses the world to do battle with us. But regardless of what weapon Satan uses or how he attempts to combat you and me, First John 5:4 declares that we have a faith that *overcomes* the world!

This means we have a faith that *overrides* and *supercedes* any organization, any event, any circumstance, or any difficult dilemma Satan would try to employ against us. He may be the "god of this world," but we have a weapon so powerful that we can shoot him down every time he shows up uninvited.

Think of what a powerful message this was to the Early Church! To their eyes, it looked as if they were no match for the Roman Empire and its demonized dictators. They were ruthlessly pursued. They were captured like wild animals. They were treated like dangerous criminals. They were even forced to fight lions, tigers, and gladiators in the public stadiums.

You and I have never had to face such a dilemma in our lives. We can't imagine how difficult this must have been for them.

Regardless of what the early believers felt or saw, the apostle John told them, "For whatsoever is born of God overcometh the world: and this is the victory that overcometh the world, even our faith" (1 John 5:4). This verse could be translated, *"You have a faith, a victory, that overcomes, masters, and champions itself even over the order of things found in the world."* In other words, John was saying, *"There is nothing your faith can't handle!"*

Although it took several centuries for this verse to be fulfilled, the Church held true to these words and believed. Finally, the entire Roman Empire surrendered to the Gospel of Jesus Christ. The faith of the early believers literally overcame the world!

Darkness tried to prevail against the Early Church but could not. John 1:5 makes it absolutely clear that *darkness does not have the ability to suppress or to hold the light under its domain.* Darkness may try to prevent the light from shining, but it never holds back the light permanently. Eventually it always comes shining through.

This is true of you and your dream, vision, or calling as well. You may feel hindered from time to time in your attempts to fulfill the call God gave you, but don't despair. Those hindrances won't last long. The only way the devil can steal your dream, vision, or calling is if you surrender to him

> **The only way the devil can steal your dream, vision, or calling is if you surrender to him first!**

first! If you hold on and refuse to give up, your faith will overcome every encumbrance the devil tries to set in your path!

SATAN TRIED TO HINDER THE APOSTLE PAUL

In First Thessalonians 2:18, Paul gives his own testimony of how Satan tried to hinder him from doing what God put in his heart. He wrote, "Wherefore we would have come unto you, even I Paul, once and again; but Satan hindered us."

The word "hindered" is the Greek word *egkopto*. This word was used to describe the breaking up of a road to make it *impassable* for travelers. This kind of *impasse* made it impossible for a traveler to get where he needed to go. As a result, the traveler's trip was *hindered*. It was *delayed, postponed, or temporarily put off*. The traveler could still take another route to get to the same destination, but the alternate route was inconvenient, cost a lot of extra money, and took precious time that could have been used another way.

By using this word, Paul informs us that demonic attacks inconvenienced him on occasion. Satan craftily sought to abort advances of the Gospel by arranging unexpected problems that delayed, postponed, and hindered the missions in Paul's heart. But did Paul sit down and cry because plans didn't work out as he intended? Did he throw in the towel and quit? *No!*

The apostle Paul never stopped just because the devil tried to get in his way! No impasse or roadblock was going to stop him! He refused to take "no" for an answer. He was going to get the job done, regardless of the inconvenience, money, time, or effort involved. He was so resolute about doing what he was called to do that he always found a way to do it.

An example of this is the time Paul left the city of Ephesus because his life was in danger (Acts 19). It could have been a devastating situation.

Paul had given three years of his life to the believers in Ephesus. When he left, he could have cried, "Oh, I don't understand why the Lord let this happen! He knows how much I love the leadership of Ephesus!" Paul could have bemoaned, "Now

I'll never see the Ephesian believers again. The devil has attacked me, and the door to Ephesus is permanently closed for me!"

But Paul understood that crying and lamenting doesn't change a thing. So instead, he went down the road to the seaside town of Miletus and rented a large facility. Then he called for the elders of Ephesus to meet him there (Acts 20:17)!

Paul figured if he couldn't go to Ephesus, why not invite the leadership to come see him? Why resign himself to defeat just because he'd hit an *impasse* in the road? Paul knew there's more than one way to accomplish a goal. So he put his brain to work and found a way to do what God wanted him to do.

Why should we stop just because the devil gets in the way? If that were the case, we might as well stop everything we're doing for the Lord right now! There will never be a time that the enemy just lets us do what's in our hearts. We must be determined to keep doing what we're called to do even if the devil tries to slam the door shut in our faces.

> We must be determined to keep doing what we're called to do even if the devil tries to slam the door shut in our faces.

So what if Satan shut the door to Ephesus? That was a good time for Paul to look for a open window! If he couldn't go to the elders, why not call them to *him*?

Paul discovered an open window in Miletus. He called for the leaders, met with them, and finished his assignment, exactly as God had ordered him to do. *Mission accomplished!*

You see, Paul had a "bulldog" attitude that refused to give up. It didn't matter how much opposition was leveled against him, he had already decided he would outlive the opposition. Somehow he'd find a way to do what God had called him to do.

PAUL, A MAN WHO REFUSED TO BE MOVED BY PEOPLE OR PROBLEMS

The events Paul encountered would have shattered a normal man. But because he used his faith and kept his focus on the prize before him, Paul was able to *override* the system and *supercede* each act of aggression that Satan engaged against him. There is no doubt that he was hindered by these devilish attacks, but they never stopped him. The devil wasn't able to stop Paul because Paul had made a commitment to be *unstoppable*.

Paul describes the difficulties and hassles he encountered in Second Corinthians 11:23-27:

> **Are they ministers of Christ? (I speak as a fool) I am more; in labours more abundant, in stripes above measure, in prisons more frequent, in deaths oft. Of the Jews five times received I forty stripes save one.**
>
> **Thrice was I beaten with rods, once was I stoned, thrice I suffered shipwreck, a night and a day I have been in the deep; in journeyings often, in perils of waters, in perils of robbers, in perils by mine own countrymen, in perils by the heathen, in perils in the city, in perils in the wilderness, in**

perils in the sea, in perils among false brethren; in weariness and painfulness, in watchings often, in hunger and thirst, in fastings often, in cold and nakedness.

Let's look at this list of difficulties for a moment so you can see what Paul faced as he carried out God's will for his life. Regardless the cost, regardless the roadblocks Satan tried to set before him, none of these difficulties ever knocked Paul out of the race. When you see the hardships he faced in the fulfillment of his life assignment, yours will pale by comparison!

Here's what Paul tells us he experienced:

In Labors More Abundant

Paul uses the Greek word *kopos* to describe the kind of "labor" he put forth in the fulfillment of his apostolic call. This word *kopos* represents the *hardest, most physical kind of labor*. It is often used to picture a farmer who works in the field, enduring the extreme temperatures of the afternoon sunshine. He strains, struggles, and toils to push that plow through that hardened ground. This effort requires his total concentration and devotion. No laziness can be allowed if that field is going to be plowed. The farmer must travail if he wants to get that job done.

This word *kopos* is the same word Paul uses to describe the kind of worker he is! He's perhaps the hardest worker he knows! In fact, he goes on to say, "In labours more abundant."

The word "abundant" is the Greek word *perissos*. It is used here in the superlative sense, meaning *very abundantly*. It would be best translated, *"I worked more abundantly than most men"* or *"I worked more than you could even begin to comprehend."*

By making this statement, Paul shows that he is not impressed by the way some preachers worked at their ministries. He sets himself apart from the lazybones in the Church world. He emphatically declares, *"When it comes to hard work, no one is a harder worker than I am!"* He has personally put out incredible energy to apprehend what Jesus apprehended him to do (Philippians 3:12).

IN STRIPES ABOVE MEASURE

Now Paul tells us that he has been physically beaten as he has fulfilled his God-given task. The word "stripes" is the Greek word *plege*. It means *to smite, to hit, to wound,* or *to violently strike.*

There are many examples of this word in the New Testament. In Luke 10:30, Jesus tells us, "And Jesus answering said, A certain man went down from Jerusalem to Jericho, and fell among thieves, which stripped him of his raiment, and *wounded* him, and departed, leaving him half dead." The word "wounded" is this Greek word *plege.*

Notice that the man's wound was so devastating that when the thieves departed, they assumed he was dead. It was *a mortal wound.* Now Paul uses this same word to describe the kinds of beatings he received as he sought to fulfill his God-given assignment in life.

This very word is used in Acts 16:33 to describe the kind of beating Paul and Silas received in Philippi. After God's power shook the prison walls and set Paul and Silas free, the keeper of the prison came to them to ask how to be saved. Acts 16:33 tells us that once the prison guard was saved, he "...took them the same hour of the night, and washed their *stripes*...." This word "stripes" is the same Greek word, *plege*. Here we see an example of the physical beatings Paul endured.

But this incident in Philippi was just one example of Paul being physically knocked around. In Second Corinthians 11:23, he goes on to say that he experienced "stripes above measure."

The words "above measure" is the Greek word *huperballo*. It is a compound of the words *huper* and *ballo*. The word *huper* means *above and beyond what is normal*. The word *ballo* means *to throw*. And when these two words are joined together, they depict a very powerful picture!

Picture an archer who takes his bow and arrows to the field for target practice. He aims his arrow at the bull's-eye, pulls back on his bow, and shoots that arrow! But he misses his target and shoots *way over the top* or *exceedingly out of range*. The arrow flies *way beyond the range of anything considered normal.*

This tells us that Paul was beaten way beyond the range of what we could even begin to imagine. The word *huperballo* describes both the *frequency* and the *intensity* of his beatings. The beatings Paul received occurred frequently. They were cruel, severe, merciless acts of brutality. What Paul's enemies did to his body was *way over the top*!

IN PRISONS MORE FREQUENT

The word "prison" is the Greek word *plulake*. It describes *a place of custody, a prison ward,* or *a place heavily guarded by keepers and watchmen.* Such a prison was usually a small, dark chamber in which the most hardened, dangerous, menacing prisoners were confined. The prisoners who were put into this particular kind of chamber were considered so risky that they were usually accompanied by a host of prison guards who guarded them 24 hours a day.

This word *plulake* ("prison") is used in Acts 12:4 for Peter's imprisonment in Jerusalem. Acts 12:4 tells us, "And when he [Herod] had apprehended him, he put him in prison, and delivered him to four quaternions of soldiers to keep him; intending after Easter to bring him forth to the people." Peter must have been viewed as especially risky to have four quaternions of soldiers assigned to keep watch over him!

Paul was also kept in this kind of extreme confinement many times during his ministry. He says he was in "prisons more frequent." In fact, Paul became so familiar with this type of confinement that he even spent his final days under similar circumstances: "And when we came to Rome, the centurion delivered the prisoners to the captain of the guard: but Paul was suffered to dwell by himself with a soldier that kept him" (Acts 28:16).

No one wants to go to jail! But if going to jail meant that Paul would accomplish his apostolic calling along the way, then that's what he would do. He was willing to undergo any inconvenience, pay any price, and go to all lengths to do what God had commissioned him to do. Even jail would not stop him.

IN DEATHS OFT

The word "deaths" is from the Greek word *thanatos*. Here, however, Paul uses the plural form, *thanatoi,* which is literally translated "deaths."

We know that Paul frequently wrote about dying. We tend to spiritualize it, but the fact is that Paul faced actual physical death on a regular basis. When he wrote, "...I die daily" (1 Corinthians 15:31), he meant, *"I am constantly confronted with the prospect of death."*

Paul faced death so often that he learned how to face it bravely. In Romans 14:8, he wrote, "...whether we die, we die unto the Lord...." In First Corinthians 15:55, we see that he learned to meditate on victory rather than mortality and fatality: "O death, where is thy sting? O grave, where is thy victory?" These are not allegorical verses about death. They are the thoughts of a man who faced the prospect of death almost on a daily basis.

Paul never sought to live under this constant threat of murder or execution. It was just a part of the journey to get where he needed to go. But rather than run and hide from imminent danger, he faced it bravely and kept moving forward to do what he was called to do.

FIVE TIMES RECEIVED I
FORTY STRIPES SAVE ONE

"Forty stripes save one" was a Jewish method of punishment, applied to Paul on five different occasions. Deuteronomy 25:2,3 refers to this method when it specifies how the wicked man should be punished: "And it shall be, if the wicked man be worthy to be beaten, that the judge shall cause him to lie down, and to be beaten before his face, according to his fault, by a certain number. Forty stripes he may give him, and not exceed...."

> Rather than run and hide from imminent danger, Paul faced it bravely and kept moving forward to do what he was called to do.

This was one of the most vicious treatments of the ancient world. The tortured person's clothing was completely removed so he appeared before his persecutors naked. His arms were tied so he could not defend himself. Then the torturer would begin to lash the prisoner's bare body with a whip made of three long cords, one from calf hide and the other two from donkey hide.

Pieces of glass, bone, and metal were often attached to the end of the cords to make the lashing more memorable. The torturer would hit so hard that the pieces of glass, bone, and metal would lodge into the victim's skin. Then as the cords were jerked backward for the next lash of the whip, those pieces of glass, bone, and metal would rip out significant amounts of flesh. This left horrid scars on the victim's body — *permanently.*

The first third of these lashes were given across the prisoner's upper chest and face, while the remaining two-thirds of lashes were applied to his back, buttocks, and legs while the victim was forced to bend over to make it easier for the torturer to hit his body. Blood flew everywhere as the cords whipped wildly through the air, making snapping noises as they struck the victim again and again.

But let's think a little deeper. If the whip was made of three cords and Paul received 39 lashes each time, that means he received 117 lashes at each beating! And he went through this grueling exercise on five different occasions, which means 585 lashes were laid across Paul's upper chest, face, back, buttocks, and legs. There wasn't a place on his body that hadn't been beaten or had pieces of flesh ripped out of it!

Paul was so committed to fulfilling his God-given call that he wouldn't let anything stop him! After being repeatedly beaten in this terrible manner, he'd get up, put his clothes back on, and go right back to what he was doing before he was beaten. He had already made up his mind. *He would not stop until his mission was complete!*

> Paul was so committed to fulfilling his God-given call that he wouldn't let anything stop him!

Being beaten was an unpleasant experience. It was definitely a part of the journey that no one would relish. But Paul refused to let this experience become a permanent roadblock to his ministry. He pushed the opposition out of the way, got up, and went on.

THRICE WAS I BEATEN WITH RODS

In the ancient world, a beating with rods was a horrible, ugly form of torture. A strong man would bind the victim's arms tightly around his body, very much as a straightjacket would do. Then while the victim's upper chest and head still lay on the ground, his legs would be pulled up into the air.

At this point, a man with a huge rod — normally made of metal — would begin whacking the bottom of the victim's feet. He would whack and whack and *whack* until the feet of the victim were bleeding, broken, and maimed. At times this beating was so severe that the victim would never walk again.

It's interesting that the Book of Acts never gives us a specific example of Paul being beaten with rods in such a manner. However, as we continue to look at this list, we'll see that many events occurred during Paul's ministry that Luke never recorded in the Book of Acts. But Paul never forgot any of them, and he tells us here about some of those events into which the Book of Acts gives us no insight.

We don't know *when* Paul's feet-beating experiences occurred, but he tells us that he was beaten with rods three different times during the course of his ministry. It's obvious that the devil didn't want this Gospel preacher to take the Gospel anywhere else! Satan attempted to maim Paul's feet to permanently knock him out of the race.

You see, the feet of a Gospel preacher are threatening to the devil. Paul quoted Isaiah 52:7 when he wrote, "…How beautiful are the feet of them that preach the gospel of peace, and bring glad tidings of good things!" (Romans 10:15). This attack on Paul's feet was an attack against the Gospel.

It is evident that rather than throw in the towel and quit because of this experience, Paul grabbed hold of the power of God, put his shoes back on, got up, and went on his way to keep doing what God called him to do. This was a man the devil couldn't keep down!

No wonder Paul wrote about the resurrection power of God! He was writing from personal experience when he said, "But if the Spirit of him that raised up Jesus from the dead dwell in you, he that raised up Christ from the dead shall also quicken your mortal bodies by his Spirit that dwelleth in you" (Romans 8:11).

ONCE WAS I STONED

This event occurred in Acts 14:19. After a successful campaign among the Gentiles in Lystra, Jewish opposers came from Iconium to stir up trouble for Paul's ministry. They were so effective in distributing bad information about Paul that the entire city turned against him. In a moment of fury, the people of Lystra stoned him and "...drew him out of the city, supposing he had been dead" (Acts 14:19).

It may well be that Paul was dead. Stoning was a malicious act. The stoners aimed their sharp rocks at the victim's head in order to deal a fatal blow. To assure the victim's death, the stoning didn't usually stop until his head was crushed. When it was apparent that there was no possibility of survival, the remaining rocks were dumped and the victim's corpse was dragged out of the city and left for the dogs and wild beasts to eat. So when Acts 14:19 says the people of Lystra "supposed" Paul was dead, there is no reason to think he was *not* dead at that moment.

Acts 14:20 tells us that as the disciples came and stood near Paul's corpse, "he rose up." Is it possible that these disciples joined hands and prayed for Paul's resurrection? This is precisely my view. Later Paul gave testimony of a visit he made to Heaven (2 Corinthians 12:1-4). He explained that he heard and saw things that he had never been given permission to speak. When did Paul make this visit to Heaven? Could it have been at the time he was stoned in Lystra? Yes, I personally think so.

No wonder Paul could write with such conviction: "For I am persuaded, that neither death, nor life...shall be able to separate us from the love of God, which is in Christ Jesus our Lord" (Romans 8:38,39). Even death cannot stop a man who is determined to keep on going!

Paul could have resigned himself to his fate as the people were stoning him and thought, *Well, I guess this is the end of the road. I guess I'll give up and die now.* If he had done that, I'm sure stoning would have been the end of him. But I'm just certain that as they stoned Paul, he thought, *I'm not dying now! My job isn't done! If they kill me, I'll just have to be resurrected!*

God can join Himself to this kind of person! God knows this is the kind of guy who is really going to get something done!

Being stoned was never a part of Paul's plan. It was an unexpected roadblock that the devil orchestrated to try to stop him from fulfilling his call. But although the experience stole time and delayed Paul's plans a little, it did not permanently hinder him from going on.

THRICE I SUFFERED SHIPWRECK

This verse is a bit of a mystery. Only one shipwreck is recorded in the Book of Acts. Yet we have already seen from this list that too many significant events occurred during Paul's ministry for all of them to be recorded in Luke's account in the Book of Acts.

Traveling by sea was a perilous and risky undertaking. Ships were not always reliable. The routes often took them through waters cluttered with sharp rocks, reefs, and debris. Even if the vessel was guided by strong and skilled leadership, currents were so strong that even the best ships could be carried directly into rocks and other dangerous obstacles.

In Acts 27:41-44, we read that Paul was traveling aboard a ship that ran into rocks and broke into pieces. In that moment of crisis, Paul became God's man on board ship! He spoke the word of faith to the crew and passengers, and soon he was in charge of the entire situation.

Once marooned on the island of Melita, he worked with the other crew members to collect wood for a fire. Apparently a venomous viper was hidden in the sticks Paul was carrying to lay on the fire. When he dropped his wood onto the flames, that snake charged out of the pile of wood and bit Paul on the hand. This type of snake was extremely poisonous. In fact, Acts 28:4 says, "And when the barbarians saw the venomous beast hang on his hand, they said among themselves, No doubt this man is a murderer, whom, though he hath escaped the sea, yet vengeance suffereth not to live."

But what did Paul do? He shook it off! Acts 28:5 says, "And he shook off the beast into the fire, and felt no harm." By the end of verse 6, the barbarian crowd was so shocked he didn't die that they assumed he was a god. *Boom!* In just a short time, Paul had the whole island gathered together for a crusade!

Publius, the chief of the island, was so impressed, he took Paul into his own home for three days. While there, Paul laid hands on Publius' father, who "...lay sick of a fever and of a bloody flux..." (Acts 28:8). The man was miraculously healed, and soon the entire island was in revival! The Bible tells us, "So when this was done, others also, which had diseases in the island, came, and were healed" (Acts 28:9). By the time Paul departed from Melita, he was so respected and honored that they "ladened" him with everything necessary for the remainder of his journey!

How would you have acted if you had been in Paul's position? What if you were shipwrecked, lost all your human possessions, found yourself marooned on an island that was inhabited by barbarians — and then were bitten by a venomous snake? Do you think you would have "shaken it off" as Paul did? Would you have turned your disaster into a revival? Or would you have been tempted to sit down and cry while you worried about your whole life being destroyed?

Paul's attitude is what kept him in the midst of revival everywhere he went. Just as you and I do, Paul had the opportunity to give into his flesh and thrown a pity party. But because he chose to keep going and never stop, God's power was always available to him in every situation.

> **Paul's attitude is what kept him in the midst of revival everywhere he went.**

In addition to this shipwreck, Paul testifies that he has been shipwrecked on two other occasions as well. These "impasses" were definitely inconvenient, but they were unable to permanently hinder him from getting to his destination.

A NIGHT AND A DAY
HAVE I BEEN IN THE DEEP

The phrase "a night and a day" refers to a 24-hour time period. The word "deep" is the Greek word *bathus*, and it refers to *the deepest parts of the sea.* Because Paul mentions this event immediately following his recollection of shipwrecks, we may assume that this night and a day in the deep was the result of one of the other shipwrecks of which we have no knowledge.

It is impossible to make much comment on this, as we know only what Paul says in this verse. Whenever and however it occurred, it was a horrific event in Paul's life. The Greek tense shows that the experience is still fresh and vivid in Paul's mind as he writes about it. The language even suggests that this is a recent occurrence.

Paul spent a 24-hour period treading water in the deepest parts of the sea. Yet it didn't scare him away from getting on the very next ship to continue his trip and go where God ordered him to go. It was just another *impasse* on the journey, but it didn't stop his trip!

IN JOURNEYINGS OFTEN

The word "journey" in Greek is *odoiporia*. This word describes a *walking journey*. The word "often" is the word *pollakis*, and it refers to *many times, often,* or *frequently*. Paul uses this phrase to tell us that he has walked to most destinations where he's been called upon to preach.

For instance, he *walked* from Antioch Pisidia to Iconium (Acts 13:51); he *walked* from Iconium to Lystra (Acts 14:6); and he *walked* from Lystra to Derbe (Acts 14:20). From Derbe, he *walked* back to Lystra (Acts 14:21); and from Lystra he *walked* back to Iconium (Acts 14:21). From Iconium, he *walked* back to Antioch Pisidia (Acts 14:21); from Antioch Pisidia, he *walked* throughout the whole region of Pamphylia (Acts 14:24); and then he *walked* all the way to Perga (Acts 14:25).

For a brief period, Paul and his team traveled by ship to Antioch (Paul's home base). But then they *walked* to Phenice and Samaria (Acts 15:3). From there, they *walked* to Jerusalem (Acts 15:4); and from Jerusalem, they *walked* back to Antioch (Acts 15:22).

From Antioch, Paul *walked* throughout the regions of Syria and Cilicia (Acts 15:41). He *walked* back through the cities of Derbe (Acts 16:1) and Lystra (Acts 16:1). Then he *walked* to

Phrygia (Acts 16:6) and *walked* throughout the regions of Galatia (Acts 16:6). After that, he *walked* to Mysia (Acts 16:8) and then *walked* all the way down to Troas (Acts 16:8).

After seeing a vision of a man in Macedonia calling to him for help (Acts 16:9), Paul took a ship from Troas (Acts 16:11). His ship ported in the city of Samothracia (Acts 16:11) but departed the next day to Neapolis (Acts 16:11). From there, Paul and his associates sailed to Philippi (Acts 16:12), a chief city in that part of Macedonia.

From Philippi, Paul *walked* through Amphipolis and Apollonia (Acts 17:1); then he *walked* to the city of Thessalonica (Acts 17:1). From Thessalonia, Paul *walked* to Berea (Acts 17:10).

Paul took a ship from Berea to Athens (Acts 17:14). From Athens, he *walked* to Corinth (Acts 18:1). He sailed from Corinth to Syria (Acts 18:18). Then from Syria, he *walked* to Ephesus (Acts 18:19). From Ephesus, he sailed to Caesarea (Acts 18:22); but from there, he *walked* to Antioch (Acts 18:22). From Antioch, he *walked* all over the regions of Galatia and Phrygia (Acts 18:23), and then he *walked* along the upper coastlines to Ephesus (Acts 19:1). The list of places where Paul traveled to fulfill his calling is amazing. Paul did a lot of *walking* during the course of his ministry!

If you add up all the miles/kilometers Paul walked, he probably spent more time *walking* than he did in *preaching.* No wonder he could say, "I thank my God, I speak with tongues more than ye all" (1 Corinthians 14:18)! He had a lot of time to pray in tongues as he walked across the east and northeast side of the Mediterranean countries to preach the Gospel and establish the Church.

This also gives us insight into the kind of relationships Paul had with his fellow travelers. It is impossible that he traveled so far, so regularly, and through such difficult circumstances without really getting to know his traveling companions. No wonder he could tell Timothy, "But thou hast fully known my doctrine, manner of life, purpose, faith, longsuffering, charity, patience, persecutions, afflictions..." (2 Timothy 3:10,11).

Keep in mind that the man who did all this walking was the same one who had had his feet beaten with rods three times! The only way Paul could have walked so extensively was if he enjoyed a healthy body. A sick man could never attempt this kind of physical exertion.

Paul *was* a healthy man. Although his feet had been beaten with rods, he suffered no remaining effects from those hideous beatings. Here again, we see that Paul knew how to draw upon the resurrection power of God to quicken his mortal flesh.

Many people today circle parking lots for 20 minutes just to look for a closer parking space. But the truth is, if they parked farther away, it still wouldn't take but five minutes to walk to their destination! People are often simply too lazy to walk unless they are forced to do it.

Paul had no car, no train, and no airplane to catch to get where he needed to go. Yes, traveling that far by foot meant he had to face incredible hardship and difficult circumstances. But nothing was so hard to bear that it was going to stop him from fulfilling the call on his life. Paul had made up his mind. Even if it meant he had to walk around the world by foot in order to fulfill his call, that is precisely what he would do.

If modern transportation had been available, Paul would have used it. Today cars, trains, and airplanes permit us to travel farther and faster. They enable us to take the Gospel to the ends of the earth. But the lack of these conveniences didn't stop Paul. Yet how frequently does lack of convenience stop us today? If lack of convenience hinders us from doing the will of God, there is a serious flaw in our level of commitment.

> **If lack of convenience hinders us from doing the will of God, there is a serious flaw in our level of commitment.**

I'm sure that as Paul traveled on these roads, he encountered literal *impasses* on roads that forced him to take unexpected, unplanned detours, costing him more time, effort, and money. Still, he pressed onward to take the message of God's Kingdom to the Gentile world.

In Perils of Waters

Now Paul begins to tell us some of the things he encountered as he traveled by foot across the countries of the Mediterranean world. First, he tells us that he was "in perils of waters."

The word "perils" is the word *kindunos*. It is the Greek word for an *extremely dangerous* or *highly volatile* situation. Paul uses this word eight times in this chapter to tell us that the majority of his ministry was encircled by extremely dangerous situations.

He basically lived in danger all the time. Danger isn't something Paul sought. It simply went with the territory God gave him.

The word "waters" is the Greek word *potamos*. It is the Greek word for *a river*. By using these two words *kindunos* and *potamos*, Paul tells us that as he traveled, he was occasionally forced to cross extremely dangerous rivers to get to the places where the Holy Spirit sent him.

Crossing rivers was a very serious act in the ancient world. It's a vivid example of the hazards a traveler encountered in Paul's time. Bridges were few and far between, especially in remote areas. This presented awkward problems, especially during times of floods and flash-flooding, which were frequent occurrences. Although Paul does not mention the exact rivers he had to cross, we know that they would have included the *Jordan River* (Judea), the *Orontes River* (Syria), the *Cydnus River* (Cilicia), the *Meander River* and *Cayster River* (Asia), and the *Strimon River* and *Axios River* (Macedonia).

During Paul's journeys, he crossed "badlands," climbed cliffs, scaled bluffs, and passed through some of the most dangerous rivers of his time. We don't usually think of these kinds of hazards when remembering Paul's ministry. But these were daily risks Paul faced to do God's will.

How many people do you know who would put their lives at such risk to do God's will?

I am always amazed at the number of people who write to my family with concern when they hear of political unrest in our nation. They often tell me, *"You and your family need to get out of there before it gets too tough! God doesn't want you to get caught in a difficult situation!"* But if the Early Church and other God-called people through the last two millenium had taken that approach, none of us would know of the Gospel today!

Regardless of what you face or what you cross through to fulfill God's plan, nothing takes Him by surprise. Certainly He didn't plan these problems. But when God called you, He equipped you with all the power, wisdom, and insight you would ever need to get across the hurdles Satan tries to put in your way. There is no *impasse* you cannot get through on your way to achieving God's will for your life!

> When God called you, He equipped you with all the power, wisdom, and insight you would ever need to get across the hurdles Satan tries to put in your way.

IN PERILS OF ROBBERS

The apostle Paul uses the Greek word *kindunos* for the second time in this text. As noted above, it is the Greek word for *extremely dangerous.*

One danger Paul constantly faced was the threat of robbers. The word "robbers" is the Greek word *lestes*. It refers to *a plunderer, robber, highwayman, bandit,* or *rapacious imposter.* This was a bad breed of bandits who used weapons, violence, and cunning in their thievery of others.

In the ancient world, robbers and thieves hid in the ditches and caves along roads that led from city to city — particularly along main routes of travel. This is why some Greek expositors translate the word "robbers" as "highwaymen." This term especially applied to bandits who ambushed those who traveled by roads. Considering how frequently Paul and his companions walked, we can easily see why Paul faced "perils of robbers."

Imagine traveling to the farthest ends of the earth by foot. You're carrying everything you need for that journey. The luggage piled on your back is filled with the clothing and cash you need for your journey. You know that pillaging, predatory plunderers are hidden in the ditches and caves along the roadside as you pass by, just waiting for the right prey to come by. You also know that these bandits are famous not only for stealing, but for wounding and killing their victims. Yet there's no other road for you to take if you are going to get where you need to go.

You can be sure that Paul and his traveling companions were alert the whole time they traveled on those roads. I'm sure they took authority in the Spirit and bound the evil forces influencing the bandits who lay in the ditches and caves, waiting for them to come along. Because Paul uses the word *kindunos* ("perils"), we know this was an extremely dangerous predicament.

Yet even this danger was not strong enough to stop Paul from doing the will of God. He bound the devil's strategies against him in Jesus' name and walked on bravely, even through dangerous places that others dared not go.

In Perils of Mine Own Countrymen

Now for the third time, the apostle Paul uses the word "perils" (from the Greek word *kindunos*, meaning *extremely dangerous*). The phrase "mine own countrymen" comes from the Greek word *genos*. The word *genos* is where we get the word "genes."

This word would be used *only* to denote *someone with whom
one shares a common ancestry.* Paul is referring to the Jewish
people who constantly opposed him everywhere he went. They
opposed him in Salamis (Acts 13:8), Antioch Pisidia (Acts 13:45,50),
Iconium (Acts 14:2), Lystra (Acts 14:19), Thessalonica (Acts 17:5-9),
Berea (Acts 17:13), Corinth (Acts 18:12-16), and so on.

Paul tells us that what he faced from his own natural
kinsmen was extremely dangerous. They persecuted and hunted
him down everywhere he went. They were the primary tool
Satan used to pester Paul. As you will see later in this chapter,
these angry, unbelieving Jews were *the thorn* in Paul's flesh that
Paul later wrote about in Second Corinthians 12:7.

But in spite of their endless persecution, the apostle Paul
pressed onward toward the high calling of God in Christ Jesus.
He wasn't going to let any group of angry religious people keep
him from doing what he was assigned to do. This *impasse* would
not stop him either.

In Perils of the Heathen

The apostle Paul uses the word "perils" for a fourth time.
Again, it is the word *kindunos,* denoting something that is
extremely dangerous. The word "heathen" is actually the Greek
word *ethnos.* It specifically refers to *Gentiles* or to *anyone not
Jewish.*

The Gentile world was a strange and curious world. It was
filled with wild religious beliefs, customs, and a pagan culture
opposed and adverse to the knowledge of a righteous and holy
God. The religion of the Gentile world promoted the grossest,

most depraved, and most perverted sort of sexuality. Thousands of different gods were worshiped in pagan temples, each with its own particular style of worship. Most of these religious orders involved the use of wine and drugs to induce the worshiper into wild, mindless debauchery as a part of his or her act of "worship" to the gods.

These religions were filled with demons. As the wine, drugs, music, drum-beating, and sexual perversion of temple worship intoxicated those participating in the pagan ceremony, demonic activity became stronger and stronger in the temple. During a moment of such intensity, anything could have happened. Things could have easily gotten out of control.

At such moments, an act of aggression against Gospel preachers could have freely occurred. This environment was extremely dangerous, especially to Paul and his team as they confronted the powers of darkness and commanded these idol worshipers to repent.

The travels of the apostle Paul took him to some of the world's most pagan and demonic cities. In fact, Thessalonica, Athens, Corinth, and Ephesus are listed among some of the most pagan, demonic cities in the history of mankind. Yet this is where the Holy Spirit led Paul. It was also where he experienced his most successful periods of ministry.

> Going where it is safe and secure is not always what God wants us to do.

Going where it is safe and secure is not always what God wants us to do. The Gospel must go to every country, every city, and every village in the world. If we go only where it's comfortable and safe, none of us will ever go very far from where we live right now. Thank God for those who went before us and who pushed the powers of darkness out of the way so we can now know the glorious light of the Gospel!

Paul faced extremely dangerous situations in the Gentile world, but it didn't stop him from going to them. He was called as an apostle to the Gentiles (Romans 15:16). No danger in the Gentile world was so terrifying that he couldn't conquer it with the power of God. Paul, whom history says was small in stature, was so mighty in the Spirit that he challenged and pushed his way through the most wicked, black, spiritually dark conditions to do exactly what God had asked him to do.

IN PERILS IN THE CITY

Now for a fifth time Paul uses the word "perils" (from the Greek word *kindunos,* meaning *extremely dangerous*). How many cities was Paul chased out of during his ministry? You would think a city would be a little more civilized, but some of Paul's worst confrontations occurred right in the heart of the world's most advanced and cultured cities.

Paul most often labored in larger metropolitan areas. As an apostle, his primary calling was to establish the Church in every place he went. Therefore, the Holy Spirit usually sent Paul into large population centers, where there were many people and the potential of a huge harvest.

As is true in large cities today, such as New York, London, Moscow, and Chicago, there were dangers in the ancient cities that didn't exist in the smaller towns and villages. Paul faced these challenges courageously with the power of the Holy Spirit. I'm certain some of these challenges were financial and political, not to mention the normal stress that a person faces when he attempts to do business in a big city.

However, none of the roadblocks Paul ran into ever kept him from doing what he was supposed to do. He pressed forward and completed his responsibility in every place to the best of his ability.

> None of the roadblocks Paul ran into ever kept him from doing what he was supposed to do.

IN PERILS IN THE WILDERNESS

For a sixth time, the apostle Paul uses the word "perils" (the Greek word *kindunos*, meaning *extremely dangerous*) to explain the events he faced in the wilderness. We don't have a clue about what Paul is talking about. We can only make assumptions. The word "wilderness" is the Greek word *eremia*. It describes *a remote, isolated location* in the middle of nowhere.

Paul's travels no doubt took him through remote areas where thieves and plunderers could have easily victimized him and his companions. I'm also certain that wild beasts confronted them as they walked from place to place. Just as they faced certain dangers that were unique to the city, they also faced dangers unique to the wilderness as well. Yet Paul faced these challenges with the assurance that God's power would enable them to conquer each peril successfully.

IN PERILS IN THE SEA

Once again for a seventh time, Paul uses the word "perils" (the Greek word *kindunos*, meaning *extremely dangerous*) to describe his experiences of traveling by sea.

As we've already seen, Paul survived three different shipwrecks. Only one of these is recorded in the Book of Acts. In addition to what Luke tells us in his account in Acts, there were two other sea catastrophes that Paul encountered.

Most people who have been in an airplane crash are hesitant to ever get back on another airplane. It leaves such a mark on one's memory that this memory is hard to overcome.

Likewise, sea catastrophes were just as dramatic and memorable. It was surely a horrible experience for someone to be adrift at sea, not knowing if he'd be rescued or if he'd survive. Paul went through this type of ordeal three separate times.

I'm sure these devilish attacks at sea were designed to put in Paul such a fear of sailing that he would never get back on another ship. But if he was going to get to the various places where God had called him to minister, he had no choice.

Therefore, Paul didn't allow these occurrences to steal his joy or to determine whether or not he obeyed God. Even if it meant he had to get back on another ship and sail through dangerous waters again, he'd do it, if that was required of him in order to successfully fulfill his God-given assignment in life.

In Perils Among
False Brethren

Now for the eighth time, the apostle Paul uses the word "perils" (the Greek word *kindunos,* meaning *extremely dangerous*). This time the danger he describes is connected with "false brethren."

The Greek word for "false brethren" is *pseudadelphos.* The first part of the word is *pseudes* and carries the idea of something that is *untrue*. It could be translated *pretend, phony, fake,* or *bogus*. The second part of the word, *adelphos* is simply the word for a *brother*. Compound these two words together, and the new word describes *pretend, phony, fake, bogus brethren*.

Paul remarks about these bogus believers in Galatians 2:4,5: "And that because of false brethren unawares brought in, who came in privily to spy out our liberty which we have in Christ Jesus, that they might bring us into bondage: To whom we gave place by subjection, no, not for an hour; that the truth of the gospel might continue with you."

These "false brethren" in Jerusalem were in fact genuine brothers who had false motives in their dealings with Paul. They projected one impression, but in reality their intentions were very different from what they projected. They were "false" because they pretended to be in agreement with Paul's doctrine. In actuality, they wanted to take Paul's converts and revert them back to legalism. Paul's emphasis is not that they were unsaved, but that they were "false" with him.

Notice the phrase "came in privily" because it describes how bogus believers behave. It comes from the Greek word *pareisago*. This word is a triple compound, comprised of the words *para, eis,* and *ago.*

The word *para* means *alongside.* It denotes something that is *very close,* such as a *para*site. The second part of the word — the word *eis* — means *into* and conveys the idea of *penetration.* Finally, the third part of this compound is the word *ago.* It simply means *I lead.*

When all of these are compounded together, the word *pareisago* ("came in privily") conveys the idea of *smuggling something in undercover.* Literally, it is a picture of someone who is *leading (ago) something into (eis)* the Church *alongside* of themselves *(para).* It is the idea of *covert activity.*

The last part of this compound — the word *para* — indicates that the false motives of these false brethren are held so secretly that they sneak them right into the midst of the Church undetected. By keeping their hidden agenda close to themselves, they are able to worm their way right into the Church leadership. Once they gain position inside a particular group, they start their destructive work from deep within the Church itself.

We know that Paul was constantly accosted by Judaizers, who came to spy out his light in Jesus Christ. It is also known that both the government and the religious leaders of the day would train and disguise specially trained agents to invade the Church. Using tactics similar to the Russian KGB of old, these agents would be so well camouflaged that they sounded like believers, looked like believers, and were often perceived to be real brethren. But in reality, they were imposters who had been sent to discover the location of church meetings. They'd inform the local authorities of the location; then the next time the church met, the police would arrest those who had gathered for worship.

Whoever these "false brethren" were, Paul said they were perilous to him. They created a situation that was *extremely dangerous* and *highly volatile*.

You can imagine how paranoid this situation could have made Paul, knowing that pretenders were out there constantly trying to secretly hurt him and those he loved. It could have driven Paul into a pattern of fear and suspicion. But instead, he relied on the Holy Spirit to give him clear discernment so he could recognize who was real and who was not. In the example given in Galatians 2:4, Paul was able to recognize their false motives and didn't even give them a single hour of his time.

Living in these types of stressful circumstances, Paul had a choice. He could either back up into insecurity or take hold of the Spirit's help to press forward.

Paul chose the latter. He refused to let these "false brethren" become a stumbling block in his life and ministry. He didn't stop making new relationships just because some of them might have been "pretend brothers." Instead, he trusted the Holy Spirit to help him make right choices. This *impasse* didn't stop him from going on to work with people, nor did it stop him from establishing the Church in various locations.

IN WEARINESS

The Greek word for "weariness" is *kopos*. It refers to *the hardest kind of work*. It is the same word Paul uses in verse 23, when he said that he experienced "labours more abundant." By repeating this word two times in this chapter, Paul is loudly sounding the bell, drawing our attention to the fact he was an *extremely hard worker*.

Paul was not afraid of hard work. There was no clock to punch with his time card, nor any employee's manual to specify how many days of vacation he got each year. Paul's whole life was his calling. He couldn't separate who he was from what he was called to do. His identity and purpose for living was wrapped up in the life assignment God had given him.

> Paul's whole life was his calling. He couldn't separate who he was from what he was called to do.

IN PAINFULNESS

To make sure we comprehend how far Paul was willing to go when it came to hard work, he goes on to say "in painfulness." This word "painfulness" describes the incredible effort, toil, or physical exertion he put forth to fulfill God's calling on his life.

The Greek word is *mochthos*. This word has to do with the idea of *struggle*. But this isn't a physical struggle with pain resulting from sickness. The word *mochthos* is the picture of *a person who has worked so hard that he is about to collapse*. He is exhausted from physical labor.

You could say that this person is physically worn out; he has overdone it. His job demanded a level of physical commitment that was beyond what is considered normal. But to get the job done, he kept pushing, pushing, and *pushing* himself further and further. Like it or not, it wasn't a time to rest. It was a time to *toil*.

Now Paul uses this word to further amplify how he works in his ministry. You see, ministry wasn't a job that Paul worked from 8 a.m. to 5 p.m., Monday through Friday. Rather, Paul's entire life was consumed with and committed to fulfilling what God called him to do. It was the driving motivation of his life and the purpose for his existence.

The *King James Version* calls this type of hard work "painfulness," but that isn't the best translation. The only thing "painful" about Paul's consuming drive to obey God was what it doled out to the flesh, which always wants to take an easier, lazier course of action.

A better translation of *mochthos* would be *to work yourself into a frazzle* or *to work yourself until you are physically depleted of strength*. This is the picture of an individual who is dog-tired and drained and who feels like his physical strength is nearly used up.

But Paul isn't complaining! He's rejoicing that in his weakness, God's power has enabled him to push beyond the normal capacity of human strength.

Because Paul had a heart to never fail or give up, God's power came upon him and empowered him to do what other men and women could not physically do. Even physical weariness was not a strong enough impediment to stop this man of God.

> **Because Paul had a heart to never fail or give up, God's power came upon him and empowered him to do what other men and women could not physically do.**

IN WATCHINGS OFTEN

The word "watchings" is the Greek word *agrupvia*. It is probably a reference to the long nights Paul lay awake to defend himself and his team against bandits and robbers who waited to attack them in roadside ditches and caves. The word "often" is the Greek word *pollakis*, which means *many times, often,* or *frequently.*

It was very common for a traveling group to take turns at "watching" during the night. If no one stayed awake and alert, plundering robbers would come and steal all the belongings of the traveling company while they slept.

This phrase "in watchings often" reinforces the fact that traveling was extremely dangerous back then, especially at night. And because Paul uses the word *pollakis* ("often"), we know it wasn't rare for him to take his turn guarding the camp at night. It happened "often" as his team traveled from place to place.

Paul was a team player. Like everyone else on his team, he took his turn watching the campfire while others slept. This may not sound like a spiritual part of ministry, but it was a necessary part of his job if he was going to get where he needed to go so he could preach.

During the course of Paul's ministry, he had to do many things that seemed unspiritual and unconnected to ministry but had to be done so he could minister. These were often mundane, boring, time-consuming, and uncomfortable obligations. Yet without them, the real spiritual ministry could have never occurred.

If you know God has called you to do something special, don't be so high and mighty that you can't do a mundane, boring, time-consuming, or undesirable task along the way. It may not be something you relish doing. But if you don't do it, you might fail to achieve the real dream God has placed on your heart. The fact that Paul sat "in watchings often" emphatically tells us that he was willing to do anything required to preach the Gospel message God had entrusted to him.

In Hunger and Thirst

The word "hunger" is the Greek word *limos*. The word "thirst" is the Greek word *dipsos*. These words refer to *being hungry from a lack of food* or *thirsty from a lack of drink*.

This means there were times when Paul didn't have sufficient food to eat. However, there is no implication of poverty in this statement. Rather, Paul recalls times of inconvenience when food may have not been available.

Paul no doubt traveled occasionally through inhospitable, barren terrain where food was not abundant. Also, because of the great distances between some of the cities Paul and his team walked to, they sometimes simply ran out of food because it wasn't always possible for them to carry enough for their journey.

Yet this lack of food and drink did not affect Paul's desire to go onward to the next town. It was only an inconvenience — not enough to hinder him from pressing ahead.

IN FASTINGS OFTEN

The word "fastings" is the Greek word *nesteia*. It refers to *skipping or foregoing meals voluntarily* — in this case, probably because there was no time to eat. The word "often" is *pollakis*, and it means *many times, often,* or *frequently*.

The apostle Paul kept a rigid routine and busy schedule. Eating food was obviously not a high priority on his list of things to do. First and foremost, he wanted to accomplish his God-given objectives for each day and each city where he labored. This doesn't mean Paul was against eating. It simply means his thoughts and focus were not on the comfort of food.

I know that when I travel to hold leadership meetings and crusades in the territory of the former Soviet Union, I am so focused on what I am called to do that personal comforts are always a last consideration. I frequently forget to eat because I am so consumed with the work before me. This is the kind of "fastings often" Paul makes reference to in this verse. Eating was not on his mind.

I have personally known many people who took a mission trip and then swore they would never take another one because they didn't like the food they were given to eat on the trip. I am astonished when I see a believer so finicky about what he eats that it steals his joy in the present and affects his obedience to God in the future.

It perplexes me when people bewail that the food doesn't taste like food "back home." Of course it doesn't! They're not home! Then after grumbling about the food, they go to an evangelistic crusade where they expect to exercise spiritual authority to cast out demons. But how in the world do they ever think they'll have power over demons if they don't even have enough power to be thankful for a meal that's placed in front of them?

"In fastings often" tells us something about Paul's priorities. He didn't take his trips to taste and experience the local menu. He went to get a job done. Good food or bad food, he went where the Lord told him to go. Time to eat or no time to eat, he was determined to succeed at the job he was given to do. Nothing as insignificant as food had the power to knock this man out of the race.

IN COLD AND NAKEDNESS

This phrase could refer to many instances in Paul's life. For instance, he may be remembering the "cold" he felt as he treaded seawater after one of his three shipwrecks.

Paul may also be remembering the "cold" he felt during one of his many imprisonments. Ancient prisons were notorious for being damp and cold. Prisoners often contracted terrible cases of lung disease and died prematurely on account of these damp conditions. To make a prisoner's stay in prison even more miserable, the captor would often strip him almost naked before throwing him into the cave-like cell.

One expositor suggests the phrase "in cold and nakedness" may be Paul's recollection of times when bandits successfully robbed him and his team as they traveled from city to city. It isn't possible to state definitely what Paul is referring to in his statement about "cold and nakedness." But whatever event he is remembering, it's obvious that it was *not* a pleasant experience.

EVERYONE RUNS INTO OBSTACLES AND DIFFICULTIES

I'm telling you about Paul's experiences because I want you to know that *everyone* runs into obstacles and difficulties — *even the apostle Paul with all his God-given revelation and anointing!*

Rather than wait for a perfect situation before you step out in faith, listen to the Holy Spirit for His timing. If the Holy Spirit says, *"Do it now,"* then you need to do it *now,* even if the surrounding environment seems difficult or unfavorable at the moment.

You can be sure that the devil will do his best to hinder what God puts in your heart. But like the apostle Paul, you have to

> I guarantee you that if you freeze every time the devil throws a roadblock in your path, you'll spend most of your life frozen.

determine that you're going to get the job done, regardless of the way you have to do it. Just because Satan hindered Paul doesn't mean he threw in the towel and quit. He did *not* quit! He just found another way to get the job done!

I guarantee you that if you freeze every time the devil throws a roadblock in your path, you'll spend most of your life frozen. Perfect circumstances are terrific if it's possible to line them up, but don't depend on it. Perfect circumstances or not, you have to decide to grab hold of God's power and move full steam ahead. God will show you how to get around that *impasse* so you can finish the job.

When Paul wrote that Satan *hindered* him (1 Thessalonians 2:18), he also had another very important picture in his mind. The word "hindered" is the Greek word *egkopto*, which describes *an impasse*, as we have already seen above. But the word *egkopto* was also used in another way.

This word was additionally used to depict a runner who is running with all his might and energy, pressing forward toward the finish line. As the runner arches his body forward toward the goal, another competing runner runs up close alongside him and tries to *elbow him out of the race.*

Of course, any competing runner who behaves like this isn't playing fairly. So by using this word, Paul warns that Satan doesn't play fairly. He will do everything in his power to cut in on you. If he can't cut in on you, he will do everything he can to elbow you out of the race.

If you feel the devil's elbow poking you in the side to force you off track, just slap the wits out of him by speaking the Word of God and pleading the blood of Jesus in his face! James says, "…Resist the devil, and he will flee from you" (James 4:7).

WHAT TRIGGERS A DEMONIC ATTACK?

What triggers demonic attacks against you, your dream, your vision, your calling, your business, your family, your church, or your ministry? What makes the devil so upset that he rises up to resist you and your efforts? If God chose you, why are you experiencing so many hassles and difficulties along the way to fulfilling your dream, vision, or calling?

> If God chose you, why are you experiencing so many hassles and difficulties along the way to fulfilling your dream, vision, or calling?

In Second Timothy 1:11,12, Paul gives us incredible insight into what triggers a demonic attack. He says, "Whereunto I am appointed a preacher, and an apostle, and a teacher of the Gentiles. For the which cause I also suffer these things…."

In this verse, Paul writes about his specific calling in the Body of Christ. He affirms to us that he is called and appointed to be a preacher, an apostle, and a teacher of the Gentiles. Then notice that he immediately follows by saying, "For the which cause I also suffer these things…" (v. 12). This follow-up statement is Paul's explanation for all the hassles and difficulties he has encountered over the years.

Satan was terrified of Paul's calling! The reason Paul was recurrently attacked is that the devil was fearful of the enormous progress Paul would make if he had no opposition!

It's almost as though Paul is saying, *"If you want to know why I've suffered so many crazy things during the course of my ministry, it's that I am appointed a preacher, an apostle, and a teacher of the Gentiles."*

Satan was terrified of what would happen if Paul operated 100 percent in his call. If Paul was able to do the incredible things he did for God's Kingdom in the face of such opposition, what kind of Gospel advancements would he make if there were no opposition? This thought was so petrifying to the devil that he threw every possible obstacle in Paul's path to slow him down, discredit him, destroy his friendships, and, if possible, to even kill him. *Satan hated the call on Paul's life.*

The reason Paul was *never* defeated by these attacks is that *he made a decision.* He decided he would not stop or give up until he had apprehended that for which Christ Jesus had apprehended him (Philippians 3:12).

Likewise, the only way you'll be able to resist the devil's attacks and successfully achieve all God has called you to do is by determining *never* to stop until you have accomplished what He put in your heart to do. Jesus taught that those who "endure unto the end" are the ones who will receive the prize (Matthew 24:13).

Determination is a key factor in finishing one's race of faith. Of course, no one can do it without the power of the Holy Spirit, but neither is the power of the Holy Spirit enough by itself. For that power to be effective, it must work in a committed person.

> Determination is a key factor in finishing one's race of faith.

God's power works in people who have *resolve.* It works proficiently through people who have decided they will never turn back until the assignment is finished. God delights in using people who are *steadfast* and *unmoving* in their conviction. He takes pleasure in those who have *stamina, spunk,* and a *doggedness* to hold on to the vision God put in their hearts and who are *tenacious* and *diehard* in their commitment.

YOU ARE THE ONLY ONE WHO CAN MAKE YOU QUIT

When I hear of people who didn't make it all the way to the end, the reason most often is that they weren't *totally committed* to do the task assigned to them. Maybe they tried it or gave it a shot, but their commitment wasn't diehard, and that's why they didn't make it.

There are many things Satan can do to try to elbow us out of the race, but the only one who can decide to *quit* is you or me.

> *Satan can't make us quit.* **That choice lies in our hands alone.**

Satan can't make us quit. That choice lies in our hands alone.

If you make the decision to stay in faith and slug it out with the power of God at your side, you can do exactly what God called you to do. But you must begin with a rock-solid, hardcore decision to do it and to keep on doing it until it's done.

God's Spirit will dress you with the power and equipment you need to accomplish the job He's given you to do. Colossians 1:29 speaks of a divine power that works mightily in those who keep striving toward the goal God gave them. But the requirement for this power is *your decision* to never draw back. This is what qualifies you for a supernatural flow of God's power. Make a lesser choice, and you will never fulfill your God-given purpose.

QUESTIONS FOR PERSONAL GROWTH OR GROUP DISCUSSION

1. Think of some specific examples of how Satan uses the different aspects of this world system — education, politics, media, etc. — to exert his influence and impose his way of thinking on people who are ignorant of his schemes.

2. Can you think of times in your life when the enemy used certain people or circumstances to block your forward progress in God's plan for your life? How successful was the devil in achieving his goal to obstruct and defeat you at that time in your life?

3. The next time the devil attempts to throw an obstacle in your way, what can you do differently to ensure a more successful outcome?

4. Have you ever failed to do what you knew God was telling you to do because the price seemed too high or His request was too "inconvenient"? Compare your level of commitment today to that particular time in your Christian walk.

5. In what practical ways can you apply to your own life Paul's example of total commitment to his divine call?

Say Yes!

NOTES:

_____

_____

_____

_____

_____

_____

_____

_____

_____

_____

_____

_____

_____

_____

_____

_____

_____

_____

_____

_____

_____

_____

CHAPTER 3

If God Chooses You,
He Expects You To Get Something Done!

By the time we finished constructing our big church building in Riga, Latvia, in 1998, I had battled principalities and powers for three full years to bring the building to a place of occupancy. Only God knows how hard I fought with my faith, prayed in the Spirit, worked against all the odds, and gave 1,000 percent of my attention to make this dream a reality. When it was finished, I was *physically tired.*

When the congregation moved in and settled into their new church home, I gave a sigh of relief. I felt myself "letting down." In truth, I was physically exhausted. But I knew that if I didn't guard myself, my flesh would dive headfirst into a pool of lukewarm water that would nullify the victory we'd just won!

I felt my flesh trying to lull me into a state of "let's kick back and do nothing but sit around and congratulate ourselves on how great our achievements are." Yes, a great thing had been accomplished. It was all right for us to celebrate about it and enjoy the victory we'd attained. It was even all right for me to take a little rest. *But I knew my flesh!* And I knew it didn't want *only* to celebrate. It wanted to *vegetate!*

Every day I preached to myself, *Stop congratulating yourself that you have a marvelous new building. It's great that this building has been built. A lot of faith and sacrifice went into this project. But if you stop now, you have failed. Now it's time to fill it with people. Your job is only half finished.*

You see, I've observed through the years that a major tool the enemy uses to keep people from achieving the big victories is to get them stuck on *small* victories. They are so proud of what they've already done that they camp out at a low-level victory and never scale the mountain in front of them to obtain a view of what God really wants them to do. They stop on the foothills when the highest mountain peaks are still before them.

You're not there until you're there — so keep your focus! Stay on track! Don't get sidetracked by a low-level victory!

It wasn't long until the Lord began speaking to me loud and clear about the next assignment He wanted to give me. He said, "Well done, Rick. Now that you've proven yourself in this small thing, I'm ready to start giving you some serious assignments. Get ready, because I'm about to give you the most strategic, important assignment I've ever given to you."

My flesh didn't want to hear that what we had done was "a small thing." But compared to what God had in store for me — moving my family to Moscow, Russia, to start a new church in the very heart of that strategic city — our recent accomplishment was just a stepping stone. Building that massive building in a former communist country was just proving ground designed to reveal if I was ready for the big projects down the road. God was watching to see how I'd do. How well I carried out the last assignment determined whether or not I'd receive the next one.

My flesh wanted to luxuriate and bask in the glory of what we had accomplished. I wanted to relish the newness of our building every moment of the day. I wanted to fixate on the fact that we were the *first* to do this in an entire generation. *But it was time to stop patting myself on the back.* The job wasn't finished. Sure, we had won a significant battle, but the war wasn't won yet.

When the Spirit of God calls to you or me, beckoning us to rise up, put on the whole armor of God, and march ahead once again into the realm of the Spirit to accomplish something new for His Kingdom, we must tell our lazy flesh to shut up. We must put on the mind of Christ and arm ourselves to do whatever God is saying — *regardless of the challenge that may be involved.*

> We must put on the mind of Christ and arm ourselves to do whatever God is saying — regardless of the challenge that may be involved.

GOD EXPECTS YOU TO DO SOMETHING WITH THE GIFTS AND TALENTS HE GAVE YOU

In Matthew 25, Jesus told the parable of the master who distributed "talents" to his servants. A "talent" referred to *a specific measurement of money.* Let me explain to you the value of a talent of money.

In the days of the New Testament, a common worker was paid *one denarius* for a full day's wage. A talent was *6,000 denari*. This means a single talent was the equivalent of about *16 years of salary*!

In Matthew 25:15, Jesus said, "And unto one he gave five talents, to another two, and to another one...." So when the master in this parable gave *five talents* to the first servant, he was actually giving him *30,000 denari*, or the equivalent of about *82 years of salary*. And when he gave the second servant *two talents*, he was giving him *12,000 denari*, or the equivalent of about *33 years of salary*.

Finally, the master gave the last servant only *one talent*. But even this was not a small amount. By any standard, it was a huge gift. It was *6,000 denari*, or the equivalent of about *16 years of salary*.

I used to feel sorry for the man who received only one talent. It seemed so discriminatory. This man seemed to be treated so poorly in comparison to the others. But I came to realize that even he who received the least amount of money received a gigantic gift. No one was shortchanged or treated poorly. *They were all extremely blessed.*

Matthew 25:16 tells us, "Then he that had received the five talents went and traded with the same, and made them other five talents." This means he doubled his investment, turning *30,000 denari* into *60,000 denari*. He turned his investment into the equivalent of about *164 years of salary*!

It takes *hard work* to double one's money. No mention is made that this man magically made this wealth. He had to work just like everyone else. The reason his fortune increased was that he put forth the effort to make it happen.

Proverbs 10:4 says that the diligent, hard worker will be richly blessed. It was the first servant's hard work that produced this incredible financial harvest.

Matthew 25:17 goes on to tell us, "And likewise he that had received two, he also gained other two." The second servant also doubled his investment. Like the first servant, he, too, was a hard-working man. He started with two talents, the equivalent of *12,000 denari.* By doubling his investment, he now had *24,000 denari,* or the equivalent of about *66 years of salary.*

The third servant received *one talent,* or *6,000 denari.* This lazy servant dug a hole in the ground, hid his money, and waited for his master's return. Matthew 25:18 tells us, "But he that had received one went and digged in the earth, and hid his lord's money."

While the other servants were working to double their investment, this third servant did *nothing.* Is it possible that his master had previous experience with this servant's work? Had his master found him unfaithful on other job assignments? Is this why he received the smallest of all the talents? Could it be that the master didn't trust him with much more than one talent?

Regardless of the answers to the above questions, we know for a fact that once the third servant received this trust from his master, he did nothing with what he had received. He didn't work. He didn't increase his potential. He simply rested on the fact that the money was safe and secure in a hole he had dug in the earth.

He may have speculated, *Why should I work? I have 16 years of salary saved away. I'll be able to live on this for a long time. There's no urgency to get a job or to push myself too hard. Maybe I'll do it later when the money finally starts to run out.*

The first servant turned 30,000 denari into 60,000 denari.

The second servant turned 12,000 denari into 24,000 denari.

The third servant just hid his money in a hole.

If these first servants were capable of doubling their money, the third servant could have done it too. *He could have turned his 6,000 denari into 12,000.* Rather than making something of himself, he squandered his time and life away by doing nothing valuable with himself.

THE LORD WILL RECKON WITH US WHEN HE COMES

In Matthew 25:19, Jesus said, "After a long time the lord of those servants cometh, and reckoneth with them." Pay close attention to the word "reckon" in this verse. It is a bookkeeping term that means *to compare accounts.* It would be used to portray an accountant who is putting together a profit-and-loss statement for his boss. He is examining the books to determine the real financial status of the corporation.

If God Chooses You, He Expects You
To Get Something Done!

In this parable, the master came home from a long trip. He wanted to know how these servants had fared with his money. By using the word "reckon," Jesus implies that the master wasn't satisfied to take a shallow look; he intended to search and dig until he obtained a full picture of the real situation. This was going to be a thorough investigation.

Jesus uses this parable to make us aware that one day He will come to "reckon" with us. A day is coming in your and my future when Jesus will stand before us, not as our Savior but as *our Judge.*

Revelation 20:12 tells us about the Book of Life. But in addition to the Book of Life, it says there are other books too. These other books contain records that are so vital, they are saved in the archives of Heaven. A day of reckoning will finally come when all these books are "opened." On that day, the Lord Jesus will measure what you and I actually did and will compare it to what we were actually supposed to do. You could say that He will look over the *profit*-and-*loss* statement for our lives.

The apostle Paul referred to this in Second Corinthians 5:10 when he wrote, "For we must all appear before the judgment seat of Christ; that every one may receive the things done in his body, according to that he hath done, whether it be good or bad."

Matthew 25:26,27 makes *very clear* what the Lord looks for when He looks at our personal accounts. Jesus employs the use of this parable to teach us what is eternally important concerning the Judgment Seat of Christ.

THE LORD EXPECTS TO FIND *INCREASE* WHEN HE RETURNS

The master in this parable expected *increase* when he returned. Matthew 25:26,27 says, "...thou knewest that I reap where I sowed not, and gather where I have not strawed: Thou oughtest therefore to have put my money to the exchangers, and then at my coming I should have received mine own with usury."

These servants were not ignorant of the master's expectations. They knew he expected them to reap! In fact, he told them, "Thou knewest." They couldn't feign ignorance. They *knew* he expected them to do something significant with what had been entrusted to them.

This master would accept *no excuses* for a lack of increase. It didn't matter how difficult the situation, how many odds were against them, or how impossible it seemed, he still expected *increase*. His servants understood that this was his expectation.

In Matthew 25:21, the master returned and discovered that the first servant doubled his investment. When the master saw this *increase*, he said, "...Well done, thou good and faithful servant: thou hast been faithful over a few things, I will make thee ruler over many things: enter thou into the joy of thy lord."

In verse 23, the master was similarly thrilled when he found out the second servant had doubled his investment as well: "His lord said unto him, Well done, good and faithful servant; thou hast been faithful over a few things, I will make thee ruler over many things: enter thou into the joy of thy lord."

But why did the master call their success a "few things"? Their accomplishment wasn't small. As a matter of fact, it was *huge*. Yet the master said to the first two servants, "Thou hast been faithful over a few things."

On one hand, the master commended them. On the other hand, his words "over a few things" seem to indicate that what they'd done wasn't such a big deal after all. I'm sure the servants were dumbfounded. What did their master mean? Was he *belittling* what they had accomplished?

What the first two servants had achieved was fantastic, but it was just the *beginning*. They had proven themselves to be hard-working and capable. They had demonstrated responsibility. The master now knew they could be trusted with true riches. Because these two stewards had proven themselves faithful, the master saw a bright future ahead for them.

> A day is coming in your and my future when Jesus will stand before us, not as our Savior but as *our Judge.*

As is always true with God, faithfulness resulted in promotion and greater responsibilities. The first two stewards had passed a test on a lower level. Now their master was satisfied to thrust them upward into even more monumental life assignments.

THE NONPRODUCTIVE SERVANT — 'WICKED, SLOTHFUL, AND UNPROFITABLE'

The servant who did nothing with his talent found himself in a horrible predicament. First, his master called him, "Thou wicked and slothful servant" (v. 26). Then in verse 30, his master called him "the unprofitable servant."

Before we go any further, we must stop to examine these words. These words vividly express Jesus' sentiment toward people who possess great potential but never develop it.

Let's look first at Matthew 25:26, where Jesus calls the nonproductive servant, "Thou wicked and slothful servant." The words "wicked and slothful" are taken from the single Greek word *okneros*. This word means *lazy* or *idle*. It carries the idea of *a person who has a do-nothing, lethargic, lackadaisical, apathetic, indifferent, lukewarm attitude toward life.*

This explains Jesus' words in Revelation 3:16, where He tells the church of the Laodiceans, "So then because thou art lukewarm, and neither cold nor hot, I will spue thee out of my mouth." Jesus was saying, *"Because you have a do-nothing, lethargic, lackadaisical, apathetic, indifferent, lukewarm attitude, I will spew you out of my mouth."*

The word "spue," or "spew," is from the Greek word *emeo*. It describes a person who is *nauseated, sickened, and repulsed to the point that he or she begins to heave and retch, regurgitating and vomiting up the revolting pollution that made him or her sick.*

This Greek word *emeo* ("to spew") used in Revelation 3:16 is the strongest word that could have been chosen to tell us how Jesus feels toward those who are *apathetic* and *lethargic* about their spiritual lives and life assignments. Jesus has no taste for *lackadaisical* people. People who are *lukewarm* about their God-given abilities or who are *indifferent* about the assignments He has entrusted to them leave a sickening taste in the Lord's mouth. *There is no other way to interpret Jesus' words in Revelation 3:16.*

Then in Matthew 25:30, Jesus calls this nonproductive servant "the unprofitable servant." The word "unprofitable" is from the Greek word *achreios*, which means *useless*. A literal translation would be *the good-for-nothing servant*.

This word describes a person whose existence in life is absolutely *pointless*. He is an aimless, purposeless person who contributes nothing to life. This person's value has never been realized because he does nothing but take up space on the face of the planet.

> **Significance is not achieved by simply existing.**

Like everyone else, this person had a choice and could have become something significant if he had used what was entrusted to him and had done what God asked him to do. But significance is not achieved by simply existing.

FINDING YOUR TRUE SIGNIFICANCE

True significance is achieved when you know that you used what God gave you and that you did what God asked you to do.

No matter how large or small the task, no matter how big or tiny the assignment, joy and satisfaction come only from accomplishing what God wants you to do. This imparts *true significance* to any person's life. It imparts a feeling of *contribution.* No satisfaction compares with this satisfaction. It is those who contribute nothing to life who usually struggle with a sense of purposelessness.

> Joy and satisfaction come only from accomplishing what God wants you to do.

Even if you think your gifts are small in comparison to others, *you can still use them*! If you use the gifts God gave you, they will increase. And the more proficient you become at using them, the more valuable you become to your family, your church, your business, and your friends. By ignoring the gifts God gave you and minimizing the life assignment He entrusted to you, *you* will cause your life to be inconsequential. A person's life becomes *pointless* when he or she contributes nothing to the world.

Don't let that be you! God didn't bring you into the world so you would be pointless and inconsequential! He has a purpose for your life. *He wants to use you!* He wants you to be a significant part of His plan.

The Bible teaches that God had plans for you long before your parents conceived you. *He was making plans for you even before you were formed in your mother's womb!* In fact, God chose you *before* the first layers of the earth's foundation were laid (Ephesians 1:4).

Think of it! Before there was an earth or any part of creation, God was already looking into the future, anticipating your life. Jeremiah 29:11 declares, "For I know the thoughts that I think toward you, saith the Lord, thoughts of peace, and not of evil, to give you an expected end."

David said in Psalm 139:15,16 that God's eyes were on you even in your mother's womb: "My substance was not hid from thee, when I was made in secret, and curiously wrought in the lowest parts of the earth. Thine eyes did see my substance, yet being unperfect; and in thy book all my members were written, which in continuance were fashioned, when as yet there was none of them."

When your flesh rants and raves that you're not worthy enough to be used, you need to take authority over your flesh and tell it to shut its stupid mouth! You need to say, "God planned a great future for me. He wants to use me. I'm not going to listen anymore to this foul garbage from my lying flesh and unrenewed emotions. I have an awesome destiny! As a matter of fact, I'm a significant part of God's plan."

Don't listen to your filthy, stinking, lying, fibbing flesh anymore! You are *exactly* the person God wants to use. And if you're not used by God, it's only because *you* didn't accept His assignment and make the necessary changes to flow with His program. He's calling out to you all the time, saying, *"Get up and jump in the race! I want you. I'm calling you to be a part of My team."*

> If you're not used by God, it's only because *you* didn't accept His assignment and make the necessary changes to flow with His program.

There is too much at stake for you to make the mistake of sitting around and feeling sorry for yourself. There is too much to lose by stagnating in a pool of bad memories where you constantly reflect on all the bad things that have happened to you. There are *reasons* for your current situation, but there are no excuses. *There are no excuses!*

EXCUSE-MAKING WILL SHACKLE YOU FOR THE REST OF YOUR LIFE

Stop thinking about all the strikes that are against you. It's high time for you to start meditating on the incredible favor that's on your side. Anyone with as much God-given favor as you have should be successful in any venture undertaken!

You have too much going for you to be sidetracked by low-level accusations of the flesh. It's a pity to think that you'd *ever* sit around and moan and groan about how bad your situation is. Even if your situation is really bad, you have to *get over it!* You have the power of the Holy Spirit. It's time for you to rise above your circumstances, crucify your flesh, and release God's power in your life to take you to a higher realm.

I never cease to be bewildered by the excuses people make to justify why they *can't* change. As a Christian broadcaster who has received several million letters from television viewers, I'm certain I've heard almost every excuse that keeps people locked up in a prison of depression and defeat.

I've learned that the flesh likes to lock on to bad experiences or past deficiencies as a reason for why it can't change. But these *reasons* become *excuses.* And until a person stops embracing those excuses as reasons for failure, he or she will never walk free from that prison.

Freedom comes to you only when you choose to let loose of your grip on the past, permanently lay aside your excuses, and turn your eyes toward the future.

The first step a person must make to get out of the invisible prison of excuses that has held him captive his entire life is to renew his mind to the truth. Breaking out of that prison cannot be an emotional choice, because emotions rise and fall like the waves of the sea. If a person is to walk free and *stay* free, he *must* choose to walk away from his excuses for failure and never pick them up again.

> If a person is to walk free and *stay* free, he *must* choose to walk away from his excuses for failure and never pick them up again.

That means we can't justify our failures anymore. We can no longer exempt ourselves from changing and doing something significant with our lives. Lame excuses no longer work, such as:

- "At a very young age, I felt unloved, rejected, and unwanted."

- "My parents were from dysfunctional homes and didn't know how to show me the love I needed."

- "My father (or mother) was an alcoholic, and, as a result, our needs were ignored so he (or she) could buy beer."

- "I was physically abused when I was younger. I've never gotten over it. In fact, I'm still so wounded that I can't carry on a normal relationship."

- "No one ever told me 'I love you' when I was young."

- "Kids at school called me names. It affected my self-image because it hurt me so deeply."

- "My husband has never treated me right."

- "I've worked hard and given my best to my job, but I've never been promoted or treated right by my employers."

- "My baseball coach showed unfair preference to others and discriminated against me. Ever since, I've felt like a loser."

- "The girls at school and church excluded me. Because of that, I've always struggled with an inferiority complex."

- "I'm so fat and ugly. No one wants to hang out with someone who looks like me. I've tried to lose weight, but it's just a hopeless cause."

- "I'm so skinny that I look like sack of bones."

And the list goes on and on and on.

It's so important for you to grasp that there are no valid excuses that would cause God *not* to choose you! No sin, no flaw, no problem is so big that God cannot overcome it and lay His hand on your life to use you in a special way.

> No sin, no flaw, no problem is so big that God cannot overcome it and lay His hand on your life to use you in a special way.

If you've been stuck in a pattern of wrong thinking and wrong believing for some time, then it's high time for you to break free! God is speaking to you. He is calling you to a higher place where your life will be more fulfilling and productive than ever before. He is beckoning you to move out of your comfort zone. He has a plan for you that is awesomely fantastic!

Unfortunately, some people will never achieve God's will for their lives because even though they know God is pointing His finger at them, they are too afraid to let go of what has been comfortable. They're tempted to cling to that which is safe, secure, risk-free, and predictable. As a result, they wait and deliberate so long that eventually God passes over them to choose a more willing and ready vessel.

Change and transition are a part of life. It's especially a part of life for those of us who are obedient Christians, since it's very rare that God allows us to stay unchanged in one spot for long periods of time. He is constantly calling us upward to a higher level of commitment and professionalism. To make the changes

He asks of us, we *must* go to the Cross, deal with our flesh, and put aside our selfish desire to be comfortable. Only *then* can we really start the adventurous ascent to higher pinnacles of victory and success!

QUESTIONS FOR PERSONAL GROWTH
OR GROUP DISCUSSION

1. Suppose you had just learned that Jesus was returning today to reckon with you according to what you have or have not done with His Word and with your divine call. Would you be excited and joyful at that news — or would you dread that moment when He looked you in the eyes and asked, "What did you do with the dream I put in your heart?"

2. In what specific areas of your life would Jesus find increase and an abundance of fruit for His Kingdom? Would He find other areas that were barren of fruit because of past disobedience?

3. From God's perspective, what characteristics in a person's life put him in the category of "unprofitable servant"?

4. Can you think of a past experience or a perceived deficiency in your life that you've used as an excuse for not changing or for not doing something God wants you to do?

5. When negative things happen in life, how does God want you to respond so that you are propelled forward instead of hindered from fulfilling your divine assignment?

NOTES:

_____

_____

_____

_____

_____

_____

_____

_____

_____

_____

_____

_____

_____

_____

_____

_____

_____

_____

_____

_____

_____

_____

CHAPTER 4

If God Has Chosen You,
You Must Be Willing
To Change and Grow

Now let me change gears for a few moments and speak to those who are in charge of choosing leadership for their churches, ministries, businesses, or organizations. The next few chapters will include guidelines for making right choices. However, if you are not such a leader, *don't stop reading*! You'll find this discussion very informative and helpful for your own growing process as well — especially if you desire to fulfill your own God-ordained role in His Kingdom.

Often when I fly through airports on my way to meetings around the world, I stop by the airport bookstore to look for something interesting to read on my flight.

I can't count the books I've bought that I never finished. They looked interesting, but once I got into them, they were too poorly written to hold my attention. More often than not, the cover was the most exciting part of the book!

A book may have a good cover. But if it doesn't have good inward content, it won't bring you any pleasure. You can spend some time staring at the cover, but after a while even that won't hold your attention. The cover design becomes nothing more than a good sales job that sells a book with *no content* on the inside.

But what if a book has a bad cover yet also has something valuable to communicate within its pages? *That* is a correctable problem. You can give it a new cover! Dress it up! Make it look better!

You can change a book cover, but you *can't* change the book! If the book itself is bad, the only way to fix it is to completely rewrite the entire book. That would take a major investment of your time, not to mention permission from the author!

To rewrite an entire book is *difficult.* To convince an author his work is so bad that it needs to be rewritten is *almost impossible.* You have to have a great deal of nerve to look into the face of an author and tell him that his book is flawed and needs to be redone. You run the risk of greatly offending him. In fact, you'll probably be sorry you ever started the conversation!

I personally know how difficult it can be to rewrite a book. When we've sent my books to be translated into the Russian language, sometimes the resulting translation has been so poor, the editors had to redo nearly every page. The editors told me, "It would be a lot easier just to throw away this bad translation and start all over again. Writing a new translation is much easier than trying to fix this bad one."

Well, a person is like a book. If his *content* is good — if he has character, a moral foundation, something inside him that is strong enough to build his life upon — yet his outward appearance is not pleasing to the eye, *no problem*! He can lose weight, exercise, or change his appearance. He can be sent to school, dressed in new clothes, and taught how to stand, speak correctly, and look presentable to others. If his heart is right, then his outward appearance is just a cosmetic bump along the road that can be changed.

But if the person's heart is bad — if his attitude is sick or if his inward character is flawed — it doesn't matter how much he pampers his flesh to make it look better or how much time he invests to lose weight, exercise, and look impressive to others. He will still just be a good-looking, *unfit* leader.

So before wasting your time and energy on someone who may not be salvageable, *first* check the *content* in the pages of his heart.

A bad book can be rewritten, but it's a time-consuming and very expensive process. Likewise, a person with a flawed character can be changed, but it will also take time. And more than likely, if you're the one trying to help him, you will pay dearly in your life to see those changes take place. Change is possible, but the hard part is getting that person to first acknowledge the seriousness of his flaws and then to allow you to begin restructuring his moral foundation.

As you attempt to rewrite what's inside that person, you'll probably encounter opposition, resistance, pride, and intense defensiveness. You see, he's fighting back to protect himself. Just put yourself in his shoes. You would probably be tempted to do and feel the same.

If you ever encounter a person who says, "Yes, I see you're right. I'm flawed, and I need to be corrected, rewritten, and redone from the bottom up. Please go after it!" you have found a very rare treasure. When a person's heart is that open, you can move "full steam ahead." Here is someone who's about to experience the miraculous, life-changing power of God!

Most often, however, you will *not* encounter this kind of positive reception. In fact, if you're a pastor or a leader, one of your greatest challenges will be to convince a person to give you permission to redo him from top to bottom. As a leader, you'll be able to see that person's gifts and talents, but you'll also see defects that will keep those gifts from becoming what they could be.

With work, a person like that could become a great asset to God's Kingdom. *But the question is, will he be willing to submit to the fire required to inwardly change him?*

SAUL'S INWARD FLAWS

This was the problem with Saul, the son of Kish. He was talented, gifted, and potentially a great leader. However, Saul's character was so flawed that in order for him to change, major repentance and submission to the hand of God would be required.

In Saul's case, the hand of God was *Samuel.* But could Saul submit to Samuel? Could he recognize that Samuel was God's hand in his life? Would he take Samuel's words deep into his heart? Would he submit to Samuel as unto the Lord? This is what Saul was *not* willing to do.

Most flawed leaders want the power and glory connected to their position, but they don't want to surrender any control of their own souls to anyone else. They want to hold people accountable to *them*, but they don't want to be accountable to anyone themselves.

Saul was no different. He pretended to be in submission to Samuel. But in reality, his actions revealed that he wasn't submitted to anyone.

By refusing to face the truth, Saul permitted the spiritual sickness in his soul to fester, swell, and become so diseased that it destroyed his anointing, stole his peace, and made him miserable till the day he died at his own hand.

> **By refusing to face the truth, Saul permitted the spiritual sickness in his soul to fester, swell, and become so diseased that it destroyed his anointing.**

Samuel loved Saul and wanted him to be a good leader. In fact, Samuel loved Saul so much that when the Lord finally rejected Saul, Samuel cried all night (1 Samuel 15:11). After that, the memory of Saul became too painful for Samuel. The Bible says that Samuel could no longer bear to look on him: "And Samuel came no more to see Saul until the day of his death..." (1 Samuel 15:35).

Samuel mourned for Saul for some time. His dream boy, his wonder child, his first choice for Israel's king, was rotten on the inside — outwardly beautiful but inwardly empty.

It broke Samuel's heart.

A Backward Situation

On occasion my heart has been broken by people who I knew had the capacity to be good leaders, but who were unwilling to deal with areas in their lives that either limited or hindered them.

These people were talented and gifted but as stubborn as a mule. They'd be soft-hearted on one occasion and hardhearted on the next, unpredictable in their ability to follow. Maybe they'd show up; maybe they wouldn't. Like the wind, they were driven this way and then that way by their emotions and lack of resolve. We'd coax, plead, and beg them to follow our godly counsel and to change, but still they refused.

The biggest heartbreak is to know that a talented, gifted person is throwing his life away and to watch all that potential go down the drain. What a waste of human life! What a tragic loss of gifts, talents, and potential. *But if the heart isn't right, nothing else can be right.*

If a person's heart isn't pliable and changeable — if he isn't willing to see the truth about himself that he needs to be changed, rewritten, and redone — all the pleading, begging, and praying in the world isn't going to make an ounce of difference.

Many thousands of hours have been thrown away by Christian leaders who have tried to change people who didn't want to be changed. In their struggle to help these people, leaders have pleaded, cried, begged, beseeched, and prayed for these people to try harder, push one more time, and get their attitude right. Yet no matter what attempt is made to help them, it makes no difference.

Suddenly the pastor or leader takes second seat to the whims of the follower and gradually becomes the beggar. The leader teaches, instructs, encourages, prays — and waits and waits and waits. And he wonders, *Did he really listen to me? Will he do what I've asked? Will he follow this time? Will he try to do it right? If he doesn't agree, will he still put forth his best effort?*

> **Many thousands of hours have been thrown away by Christian leaders who have tried to change people who didn't want to be changed.**

Every pastor or leader knows the frustration I'm describing. There is nothing more unpleasant than to feel like you are simply hanging on, hoping that someday the person you're trying to help will wake up and begin to take your counsel to heart. How defeated you're tempted to feel when you hope again and again for that person to change, yet he consistently lets you down! One moment he says he respects you, but the next moment he totally ignores what you say.

When this kind of situation develops, all power lies in the hands of the follower as the pastor or leader becomes paralyzed in his ability to lead. All progress stops. The leader's hands are tied. He is bound by a ridiculous situation. The pupil becomes master, and the master becomes servant to the ups and downs of the pupil. It's a backward situation.

That church member needs to be talked to very strongly. In fact, he needs to be rebuked! *What an ungrateful person he is!* To think that the pastor or leader has invested his time, energy, talents, gifts, and life experience into that person, and now the person is holding the leader captive! *It's wrong, wrong, wrong!*

That church member ought to thank God for the privilege of receiving this kind of attention. It's a *great* privilege to have someone invest so much into one's life. The person needing help should understand that and be grateful. He should rise up and call his pastor or leader *blessed* for what he has done for him.

WHY DO LEADERS KEEP HANGING ON TO UNTEACHABLE PEOPLE?

As leaders, why don't we put an end to these games? Why don't we just say, *"The game is finished, and you're the loser. I'm not investing any more time and energy into you."* Why do we continue to play by people's merciless rules instead of putting an end to all these ridiculous shenanigans so we can move on to more serious-minded people?

Many times leaders keep on trying because no one wants to lose an investment. For instance, what if someone puts money in the stock market with expectations for a high yield, and suddenly the market begins to tumble? *What should that person do?* Pull his money out and lose a little, or hang on and hope for the market to go back up again?

It's natural to hope that the market will turn upward again. Even if it looks impossible, no one wants to lose even a small part of his investment. If the market takes an upward turn, those hopes can pay off well in terms of huge dividends. But if the market keeps plummeting, false hope can leave a person penniless. It's hard for a person to let go when he's put so much in and expected to get so much out.

Well, the same thing is true when you've invested so much of your life into people.

We once had a youth pastor who was one of the most gifted young men I'd ever met. But he had an attitude problem big enough to match his gifts and talents. He was prideful, unbendable, and unwilling to see any way except his own way. No one else on the staff was as good as he was, as smart as he was, or as spiritual as he was. After a while, it became almost *unbearable* to work with him.

This young man talked *down* to other people on staff. He showed no respect to anyone, regardless of how long a person had been on staff or in the ministry or what kind of price he or she had paid along the way. From the way this man carried himself and how he spoke to others, it was clear to everyone that he thought he was better than everyone else, including me. *And I was his pastor!*

When I tried to discuss these problems with him, he just sat in front of me with his eyes fixed, arms folded, back rigid, and head cocked back. It was like trying to talk an enemy into becoming your best friend. It just wasn't working.

This went on for almost two years. Other staff members began to come to me and say, "Pastor, why are you allowing this to continue? Why don't you stop this? He shouldn't talk to you like this! Why don't you remove him?"

They were right. He shouldn't have spoken to me the way he did. He had no right to ignore my instructions. It was wrong for him to talk to others as if they were beneath him. The whole situation was wrong — *extremely* wrong.

But I had invested so much of myself in him that it was hard for me to let him go. I prayed for him. I talked to him. I encouraged him. I rebuked him. I corrected him. I spent countless hours thinking of him and talking to Denise about how I could help him. Two years of my life were invested into this young man, who had as much potential as anyone I'd ever known.

I agonized over what to do. I knew it was time to let him go. But even though I knew what I *needed* to do, actually *doing it* was still very difficult. I didn't want to believe it was over.

Any leader will attest to how difficult it is to let someone go after investing so much into him. It is hard to let go simply because of the investment of *time* and *emotion* that's been deposited into that person.

YOUNG AND DUMB

Sometimes people are just young and dumb. Loaded with incredible talent that they don't see or fully appreciate, they just do the *minimal* that is required. With a little extra effort, they could go straight to the top.

As leaders, we see it. We recognize what God has in store for these young people; we see what they have the capability of accomplishing. *I have no condemnation for them, since this was my own story when I was young.*

These young people may be mightily gifted (or at least think they are!) but have no discipline. They may not even see a need to be disciplined. They may think their gift alone will cause them to succeed in life.

Many young people hope and believe that one day they will wake up, and the stars will be aligned in their favor. Then just like in a fairy tale, the heavens will open, a light will break forth and shine upon them — and they will enter center stage to become a Big Star in life.

This is the stuff fairy tales and movies are made of, but it doesn't even come close to the hard realities of life. If you want to succeed, you have to work at it. If you want to be blessed, then get out there and make yourself valuable to someone or to some organization. It's good to dream and have a vision. But without corresponding actions, it will never be any more than a dream.

> It's good to dream and have a vision. But without corresponding actions, it will never be any more than a dream.

What determines the end of the story for the "young and dumb"? Whether or not they are willing to open their eyes to the truth and make the necessary changes to make it to "center stage."

- Is this person willing to do what is required to ignite the gifts in his life?

- Does he have the guts to correct the flaws in his character so he can become a leader?

- Is he going to allow the fire of God to change him?

- Or is he going to go the way of millions of other gifted and talented people who did nothing and therefore died poor and unknown?

DEAD AND BURIED FOREVER

I shudder to think of the books that could be written about people who wasted the talent and ability they possessed to write symphonies, paint masterpieces, play musical instruments, write great books, or develop ground-breaking theories about science. Many even had the natural-born skills to lead cities, nations, and empires. Yet they died *unknown* with no credit to their name for having accomplished *anything* in life.

When their coffin was placed into that hole and the clods of dirt thudded onto its surface, hiding it from view forever, an immense tragedy took place. *Permanently buried* was a masterpiece never painted, a song never sung, a symphony never written, a book never penned, an answer for medical science never discovered, a national leader who never emerged — in short, a totally wasted life. *Nothing is more immoral than this.* No crime, no violent act is more tragic than a person who was gifted and could have made a difference but didn't.

As pastor and leader of a large ministry, I see wasted human potential all the time. It makes me so upset that sometimes I feel like taking these people by the shoulder and shaking them till their teeth rattle. Why won't they wake up and get serious about life?

Unfortunately, although this sad situation should never occur in the Church, believers are some of the most gifted lazy people in the world. Too often they are gifted both naturally and spiritually but are still making no impact. Their eternal destiny is Heaven, but in this world there is no vast difference between them and the unbelievers to whom they should be preaching. At the point of death, one will go to Heaven and the other will go to hell. But in life, they both did the same thing — *nothing.*

I can think of people who are gifted to sing but are so lazy and uncommitted that they might come to church and they might not. You can push and encourage them, and for a while it may seem like you've made a little progress. But when the smallest little problem comes along, everything you've done to encourage them collapses. It's all a facade. It's not real. You are doing all the pushing and encouraging. It's time for them to get with the program; otherwise, it's time for *you* to move your energies to someone who really has a desire to change and grow.

One evening while in London, my associate and I took a walk through London's theater district. As we strolled along the streets, we heard singing, dancing, and the sound of drums, violins, and all kinds of instruments being played on the street by musicians who couldn't get a job anywhere else.

Talent was all around us. I found myself wanting to run back and forth from one side of the street to the other in order to absorb this vast array of gifts and abilities.

These people were loaded with talent — yet they were playing on the streets! What were these kinds of gifts doing on the street? They belonged in a showcase! They were passing the hat to collect coins from bystanders who listened to them play. They were playing for a donation, a handout. After enjoying the performances for just a little while, both my associate and I became utterly *disgusted* and chose to leave.

It disgusted me because it made me think of the *less* talented people in the church whom we have to beg to serve the Lord with their gifts. We beg them to play. We beg them to come to rehearsal. We beg them to serve. *We beg and beg and BEG.*

I couldn't bear to hear that fabulous music being played on the streets by musicians working so hard to gain recognition for their gifts. They were professionals in the truest sense of the word. Those on the streets of London were far more serious about their skill than most Christians are about theirs, yet how frequently must we bend over backwards to get them to use their *lesser* gifts for the Lord.

Eventually a time comes when, as a leader, you must stop begging. If a person refuses to get serious about using his gifts and talents for the Lord, you finally have to turn to someone who may be less talented but has the desire and willingness to work.

I realize how hard it is to let go when you see so much potential in that person's life. But if he remains unwilling to let the fire of God put him through a process that will change him and bring forth the gold that's hidden within, then you can't do any more to help him.

You might protest, "But if I turn to people who are less talented in their leadership skills, it will put our church or organization under stress. We'll have to wait for their skills to rise to the top, and this will put us behind schedule. It will create a hardship for us."

This thinking is understandable, but it's also wrong. Accomplishing tasks in a manner that is slower but right never hurts your church or organization. It only makes it stronger, healthier, and better.

It's true that you may not gain ground as quickly as you wished. But when you finally gain that ground, it will really be yours. There won't be any more backtracking, redoing, or rebuilding. The infrastructure will finally be built right with the right people who have right hearts and attitudes.

Do what is right. Let this be your guiding principle when selecting leadership. If you let this be your rule of operation, you will build something that will last for many, many years to come. Even if it takes longer, it will endure the test of time.

Now that I've lived in the former USSR for so long, I am amazed when I return to visit the United States. The houses in the United States are big, beautiful, and built extremely fast. From bottom to top, a house can go up in two months, complete with electricity, windows, carpet, tiles, and parquet. *It's almost as if a house suddenly appears from out of nowhere!*

However, these houses, beautiful as they are, are built from materials that don't endure the test of time, such as wooden frames and sheetrock walls. The end result is mostly cosmetic — nothing like the houses on this side of the world that are made of rock, concrete, and plaster and endure for centuries. For instance, the apartment that is our home in Moscow is half as old as the United States of America! Built more than 100 years ago, it is older than any existing building in the state of Oklahoma where I was born and raised.

At that time the technology was slow and the process very painstaking. But the building was built right. It was built strong. It is still standing today and will still be standing 100 years from now.

You see, how we build and the methods we use determine how long our work remains. If we build fast and cheap when choosing our leadership, then that is what we're going to get — a fast, cheap work for God's Kingdom that falls when it encounters obstacles or opposition. But if we will build slower but stronger, we will establish a solid leadership team that lasts through the decades.

> How we build and the methods we use determine how long our work remains.

When you finally wake up to the fact that you're building with wrong material — with people who look good and are loaded with talent but are not teachable — then it's time for you to take action. *Don't hold on to what God has released.* It's time to let them go. You must do what God does. If God has released them, you must release them too.

It may look as if you have no other people to whom you can turn. But when you let those people go, God will open your eyes to see rich treasures in your congregation or organization you've never seen before. They are the ones who will appreciate your input into their lives. *Go after them!*

In Genesis 6:3, the Lord said, "...My spirit shall not always strive with man...." Even God eventually comes to a time when He says, *"Enough is enough."* In that dreadful moment, God withdraws from the person who refuses to change and turns His attention to those whose hearts are open and cooperative with Him.

For instance, God tried hard to deal with Esau's heart, but Esau would not be moved. Finally, God moved on to someone whose heart was right. When Esau later decided to get serious, it was too late. The opportunity had passed him by (Hebrews 12:17).

There comes a time when you must stop throwing away your time on certain people. Yes, people are precious, and we need to treat each of them as a unique creation of God. But *your* gifts are also precious.

Perhaps you've given again and again to some people, but your efforts haven't been appreciated, valued, or received. In that case, you need to respect *yourself* enough to quit giving away the precious things of your life to people who don't even care. *If that's their attitude, they aren't worthy of you.*

Don't 'Give Your Holy Things to Dogs' Or 'Cast Your Pearls Before Swine'

In Matthew 7:6, Jesus said, "Give not that which is holy unto the dogs, neither cast ye your pearls before swine, lest they trample them under their feet, and turn again and rend you." *What is holy in your life?* What was Jesus talking about when He said "Give not that which is holy unto the dogs..."?

These holy things are what God has done *inside* you. They are your spiritual gifts, the hard lessons you've learned as you've submitted to the dealings of God in your life, the insights you've gained over the years, the wisdom you have amassed as a result of years of experience. All these things are *holy* and *valuable.* It's impossible to put a price tag on that which has cost you your life. *Who can measure the tears, pain, and energy spent to gain those revelations?*

When you share these holy things, you have opened the door to your most private treasures. When you begin to share details, secrets, insights, and wisdom that you've learned through the hard knocks of life and from the Spirit of God, it is a precious gift you are giving. You should never underestimate the tremendous value God places on the experience and wisdom you've gained in your life. These are *holy* things.

Every time you break open the Word of God and share the rich treasures God has shown you — the principles, the lessons, the insights you've gained as you have dealt with your own heart and sought to do God's will — you are giving out *precious* things to those who listen.

Jesus likens these holy things to *pearls*. Pearls are not easily found. To obtain the richest, most beautiful pearls, a diver must dive again and again and again and again. Then after lifting the shells from the floor of the sea, he must force open the mouth of the shell and dig through the tough meat of the muscle, poking and searching for the tiny white pearl that was formed over a long period of time. These pearls are precious, rare, valuable, and hard to obtain.

This is how you should view the things God has done in your life. This is the value of those life experiences you have learned as you've walked with Him. Like precious pearls, they have great value in your life because they cost you something. They are not the result of shallow swimming. *You've had to go deep into God to obtain these spiritual treasures.*

Each time you open the door to those treasures and begin to share them with another, you need to remember that you're sharing your *pearls* with that person. The counsel and advice you're giving may be free for him, but it has cost you everything! If it isn't appreciated, *then stop giving that person your pearls!*

Jesus said, "Give not that which is holy unto the dogs, neither cast ye your pearls before swine..." (Matthew 7:6). Notice that He likened certain people to dogs and pigs. Both dogs and pigs are consumers. They take, take, and take. They eat and then want more. They never think to ask where the food came from, who paid for it, or what process was required to produce it. They are just mindless, careless consumers.

If you've ever been to a pigpen, then you know that pigs do nothing but lie on their sides and jump up just in time to eat. They never contribute anything to the farm until they're dead. Covered in their own mess, waddling in their own filth, they just wait to be fed again and again.

They fight and kick to see who will get to the food first. Slopping up the food, slobbering all over themselves, they "eat just like pigs." Driven to have their need for food met, they never stop to say thank you to the person who brought it to them. Not one "Thank you" is heard — *not even one*!

This is exactly like people who don't appreciate the holy things that are freely given to them from the depths of another person's life. It's sad to say, but many believers live and act just like pigs because they are careless, mindless consumers of other people's time and energy.

These people never think about how you obtained your wisdom, what it cost, or how many years it took you to come to this place of growth in God. They just take, take, and take. And after you feel as if they've drained you of all your strength, they don't even take the time to say thank you for what they've consumed!

When Denise and I first began in the ministry, we thought our door and telephone had to be available to people 24 hours a day, 7 days a week. And people came all the time. Some of them really needed help, but others were just *leeches* coming to suck the life out of us.

It didn't take us too long to learn that some people just wanted *us* — *our* time and *our* energy. They didn't have any intention of changing or doing anything we suggested. It was almost as if they were sent on a mission intended to drain us dry of everything we had inside of us.

Once these people got finished with us, they were off to someone else. We were just the ones they attached themselves to for that moment. As long as they could get just a little more out of us, they stuck around. But when they had drained us dry, they were off to find a new victim.

At first, I thought I had to be accommodating to every phone call and knock on the door. But after a while, I learned that all the counseling in the world isn't going to help some folks. They don't want to be helped!

Thank God for those who are sincere and desire to make a change. Our doors are still open to anyone who is hungry for God, who wants to be delivered from wrong thinking and habits, who really desires to know the Word of God. *Our door is open and will always be open to these types of people.*

I learned a long time ago to shut the door and turn off the telephone if it's one of those people who just wants to consume and devour my time. It's a waste of my time and energy, and it won't make any difference in that person's life anyway.

JESUS SAID THEY WILL TURN ON YOU!

Pastors and leaders from all over the world could tell you about people like this whom they've tried to help. The leaders may have begged, pleaded, cried, and waited for these people to get their hearts right. But later these same people turned on their leaders and accused *them* of being unloving!

These are the kinds of people Jesus was talking about in Matthew 7:6 when He said, "...lest they trample them under their feet, and turn again and rend you." They take from you now and then later turn against you!

It is *extremely* hard to understand how someone you have tried so hard to help can act so ugly! But that's frequently the case. As soon as you say, *"Enough is enough!"* and turn your attention elsewhere, this type of person begins to accuse: *"You are so unloving. You don't love me the way you used to love me. If you were a good leader, you'd listen to me when I talk. You just don't understand."*

You may assume that these people would *know* they are loved. The reason you endured so long is that you *do* love them. If you didn't love them, you would have let them go a long time ago. Only love could have kept you going after they disappointed you time after time.

It is time for you to take charge of that relationship. If they aren't serious by now, they probably will *never* be serious. Stop behaving like a beggar. You shouldn't have to beg anyone to follow you. You need to think more highly of yourself — and

those who follow you need to think more
highly of you as well.

People must never take you and the
pearls of your life for granted. If they do,
then stop giving to them until their attitude
changes. If their attitude *never* changes,

> **You shouldn't
> have to beg
> anyone to
> follow you.**

then find someone who *will* appreciate what you are trying to
accomplish in his or her life.

There are other fish in the sea. You are *not* locked into this
one person. Lots of potential leadership exists out there, just
waiting to be tapped into. Quit acting like the world rises and
falls on whether or not this *one* person gets with the program.
Leave him, and move on to someone who will contribute to the
program instead of just being a "taker" and a consumer of your
time and energy.

Samuel waited a long time for Saul to change. He prophesied
to Saul; he taught and corrected Saul. But still it made no
difference. It was a *lost cause*. Saul was not compatible with the
kind of character *required* for godly leadership. So the Lord
turned his attention to someone else, just as we must learn to do
when we face the same situation.

If you are a parent, pastor, teacher, or leader in any capacity,
you can easily identify with the heartbreak Samuel experienced
when he finally realized Saul wasn't going to change. All that
potential — lost. All those incredible, remarkable traits that

> Saul was a gifted man who was destroyed because of a wrong inward moral foundation.

could have made him great — wasted. Saul was a gifted man who was destroyed because of a wrong inward moral foundation.

Samuel mourned over Saul for a long time. In fact, he mourned for so long that God finally told Samuel, "...How long wilt thou mourn for Saul, seeing I have rejected him from reigning over Israel? fill thine horn with oil, and go, I will send thee to Jesse the Bethlehemite: for I have provided me a king among his sons" (1 Samuel 16:1).

DON'T REPEAT THE SAME MISTAKE

Obeying the Lord's command, Samuel arrived at the house of Jesse and began to thoroughly look over Jesse's sons to see which one the Lord had chosen to be king.

First Samuel 16:6 says, "And it came to pass, when they were come, that he looked on Eliab, and said, Surely the Lord's anointed is before him." Eliab was the oldest son of Jesse, or David's oldest brother. Outwardly he looked similar to Saul; he was tall and handsome, and his countenance was impressive. Although Samuel had just chosen a handsome man who turned out to be a failure, it appears that he was still tempted to be lured in the direction of good-looking flesh and repeat the same mistake he had made with Saul.

One of the greatest challenges for us in leadership is to not be led by what we see! Everything that glitters is not gold, and some of the finest diamonds in the world are buried under rock. We must ask the Spirit of God to give us special discernment that we might see by the Spirit who has the right inward makings to be a leader.

> **One of the greatest challenges for us in leadership is to not be led by what we see!**

Neither can we be moved by need. Just because we have an empty position doesn't mean we have to immediately find someone to fill it. Whenever we move hastily, we usually make our worst choices. It's better to wait and be temporarily inconvenienced than to install a wrong person into a position and then later have to figure out a way to remove him. If we will wait on the Lord to direct us, He will bring us the right person.

> **Most of the leadership mistakes I've personally made have occurred because I was moved by need rather than by the Spirit of God.**

Most of the leadership mistakes I've personally made have occurred because I was moved by need rather than by the Spirit of God. It doesn't take many of these kinds of mistakes (which, by the way, are often expensive even in terms of money) to learn not to do it again.

Before Samuel repeated this mistake again, the Spirit of God stopped Samuel and spoke to him: "...Look not on his countenance, or on the height of his stature; because I have refused him: for the Lord seeth not as man seeth; for man looketh on the outward appearance, but the Lord looketh on the heart" (1 Samuel 16:7).

One by one, the sons of Jesse passed before Samuel for his inspection. Seven sons passed before Samuel, but none of them were chosen of the Lord to be king. At last, Samuel asked, "…Are here all thy children? And he said, There remaineth yet the youngest, and, behold, he keepeth the sheep. And Samuel said unto Jesse, Send and fetch him…" (1 Samuel 16:11).

No one in the family thought David could be a candidate for king. He was too young. He had too little experience. He was just a small boy, not really even worthy of consideration. He was barely past the age of puberty — certainly not old enough to be used by God!

But First Samuel 16:12,13 goes on to say, "And he sent, and brought him in. Now he was ruddy, and withal of a beautiful countenance, and goodly to look to. And the Lord said, Arise, anoint him: for this is he. Then Samuel took the horn of oil, and anointed him in the midst of his brethren: and the Spirit of the Lord came upon David from that day forward. So Samuel rose up, and went to Ramah."

No one would have expected that David was the Lord's candidate. Yet this young man was precisely whom the Lord chose. The difference between David and Saul was that David had a *teachable heart*, and Saul did not.

This is a make-or-break issue when you are a leader or someone who aspires to a leadership position. The day you refuse to keep growing and developing is the day you choose to let another take your place.

As we move into the next chapter, we will look at how the Lord tests us to make sure we are ready for the next God-assignment. His calling on our lives is already a settled issue, but how can you or I know when we're ready to step into the next position of responsibility He has for us? How can those in authority over us know that we're ready?

> The day you refuse to keep growing and developing is the day you choose to let another take your place.

One thing we can know for sure — if God has chosen us for a particular task in His Kingdom, He has already tested us and knows we are ready!

QUESTIONS FOR PERSONAL GROWTH OR GROUP DISCUSSION

1. What outward signs reveal a person of flawed character?

2. What should a leader do when he has tried without success to work with a person who stubbornly refuses to change?

3. Why do so many leaders make the mistake of holding on far too long to a person who possesses talent but lacks the necessary character?

4. Have you ever "cast your pearls before swine," sharing the deep things God has placed in your heart with someone who trampled those "pearls" underfoot? What lessons did you learn from that experience?

5. What is one of the greatest challenges for a leader when selecting leadership?

NOTES:

_____

_____

_____

_____

_____

_____

_____

_____

_____

_____

_____

_____

_____

_____

_____

_____

_____

_____

_____

_____

_____

_____

CHAPTER 5

If God Chooses You,
He's Already Tested You
And Thinks You're Ready!

B efore we go any further, we must first step back a moment
to see how God *does* and *doesn't* choose people to do His
business. It's *imperative* for us to know what God counts
as most important, especially if we want to be used by Him.

God has dealt with human beings for more than 6,000 years
now. Through the ages, He has mightily used both gifted,
talented people and those who possessed little or no natural gifts
or talents.

It's interesting to note that most of those who were greatly
gifted according to the flesh were so strong-willed and prideful
that they had to be *dramatically changed* before those gifts and
talents could be used for God's glory. On the opposite extreme,
those who had no natural gifts and talents often had to be
dramatically convinced that they were worthy to be used by
God.

But whether or not a person possesses natural gifts and
talents, one principle holds true: If that person is destined to
hold a significant role in the plan of God, God will *first* purify
and prepare him for the job. The Bible is full of such examples.

God puts those He chooses through a process designed to remove any weaknesses that could later create defects in their

> **If a person is destined to hold a significant role in the plan of God, God will *first* purify and prepare him for the job.**

ministries or life assignments. After this purifying, preparing, and cleansing process is complete, His people then have the inward strength and character to withstand adverse pressures and the will to finish the job.

If you know God has chosen you, don't be surprised if you are put through fires that expose weaknesses in your character. This is God's mercy at work in your life. If He placed you in a powerful position without first removing the dross from your life, that defect would show up later and cripple your work or ministry. Thank God for the fiery experiences that cause you to see the character defects in your life so they can be dealt with and removed!

The Bible also tells us about those who were *never tested* before they were chosen. A prime example of a man who was elevated before he was tested, tried, and proven is King Saul. His character wasn't tried and prepared for such a position; as a result, his kingdom ended in disaster. Later in this chapter, we'll look at exactly what happened to him.

The Bible also tells us about others whom God called and tried to refine in order to protect them from self-destruction. But because these people relied totally on their gifts and talents and *refused* to allow God to work in their character, they were later destroyed — *even though God's plans for them had been great.*

You see, God can have all the best intentions in the world for us. But how we respond to His dealings in our lives determines whether or not His intentions for us are fully carried out.

> How we respond to God's dealings in our lives determines whether or not His intentions for us are fully carried out.

I think of Samson from the Old Testament. He's a perfect example of a gifted, anointed man who had a character defect yet refused to allow God to purge him of it.

When I was a boy, I loved the story of Samson. I even named my dog "Samson." And later when we got a cat, I named it "Delilah."

I'd sit almost hypnotized as I listened to my mother read about Samson killing a lion with his bare hands, slaying one thousand Philistines with the jaw of an ass and pulling down the temple of the Philistines. I also remember cringing when I heard how the Philistines gouged Samson's eyes from his head (Judges 13-16). It was the perfect story for a little boy with a vivid imagination. In fact, it was my favorite Old Testament story.

I was too young to realize how sad this story was. Although Samson acted like an Old Testament superman, he was no hero. *He was a terrible failure who missed his opportunity to be a real hero of the Old Testament.*

As the recipient of a special calling by God's grace and mercy, Samson had everything working in his favor. But because

> Because Samson neglected to deal with a loose attitude and a lazy disregard for a holy life, he made choices that led to the forfeiture of his life assignment.

he neglected to deal with a loose attitude and a lazy disregard for a holy life, he made choices that led to the forfeiture of his life assignment. In the end, Samson threw his life away. It was never God's plan for this gifted young man to end up dead under the rubble of a fallen Philistine temple.

Samson did not inwardly possess the kind of character that is required to be a man of God. *His inner core was wrong.* When God tried to change him, he *refused* to cooperate and played right into the hands of his enemies.

Samson's story is one of the saddest in the entire Bible. Had he submitted to the fire of God and allowed himself to be changed, he could have become a true Old Testament hero.

AN EXPENSIVE LESSON IN MY EARLY MINISTRY

When Denise and I were young in the ministry, we had a young man on our staff who was gifted in music and communication. This man had previously worked in the field of business, where he'd done well until he was accused of taking funds from the cash register. A question had been raised about his integrity, and he'd been released from his job. However, I ignored every report about his lack of integrity because I was so impressed with his abilities.

I was most impressed by his ability to sing and write music, as well as his natural abilities to influence others. Soon I asked him to join our team. This was one of the most *painful* mistakes I had made in my life up to that time. Inviting this young man to come into our inner circle was like personally inviting Judas Iscariot to betray me! It didn't take too long until I began to see what kind of person he really was. *The truth was far different from what I had first thought.*

This young man talked only about himself. He looked for opportunities to put me down when others were present. He constantly exaggerated his importance in the eyes of others. I tried to overlook these faults, attributing them to his youthfulness. I hoped he would grow out of them. But as time passed, the young man *didn't* grow out of those troublesome traits; in fact, he became *worse*.

I met with him every morning and tried to teach him principles from God's Word. But he was a classic *know-it-all*! He already knew everything! I realized I had no authority in his life. There was no foundation between us on which to build. Furthermore, he didn't seem to want a relationship. It didn't take me too long to realize he was a "careerist." In other words, he was simply looking for a way to promote *himself*.

Now, in terms of gifts and talents, this young man was everything a pastor could desire to have in an associate. Yet after a period of time, I found myself joining hands with Denise to pray for a peaceable solution to this problem. I asked God to remove him and thus deliver us from a very uncomfortable situation, and eventually God did just that. Our dreadful experience with this young man was an important lesson in my early ministry of what *not* to do — a lesson I have not forgotten and have sought to never repeat!

KING SAUL — THE PERFECT EXAMPLE OF A GIFTED MAN WITH NO CHARACTER

King Saul is the best example from the Old Testament of what I am talking about. The Bible tells us that when Samuel first found Saul, he was the most handsome, attractive young man in all of Israel. First Samuel 9:2 says Saul was "...a choice young man, and a goodly: and there was not among the children of Israel a goodlier person than he: from his shoulders and upward he was higher than any of the people."

Notice that this description of Saul refers entirely to the *outside.* It speaks of his looks and his height. It says that no other young man in Israel could compare to his outward appearance. But the verse is oddly vacant of any mention of Saul's heart, attitude, or character. Instead, the word "goodly," meaning *an outwardly handsome appearance,* is used twice in this verse. This tells us that Saul had a lot more going for him on the *outside* than he had on the *inside.*

If it was a worldly king that Israel was seeking, Saul was the perfect choice with his tall, broad shoulders and striking appearance. But as time passed, it became evident that this handsome man had little inward character upon which to build his kingdom. The flaws in his character would prove to be spiritually fatal in just a short period of time.

These flaws were so serious that God took the kingdom from Saul and gave it to another man who was younger, less experienced, and less educated — but who had a *right heart* toward God. David had such a strong inward character, God bypassed all the other older, more experienced candidates and chose him to be the second king of Israel.

WHATEVER IS INSIDE YOU EVENTUALLY COMES OUT OF YOU

One thing we learn from King Saul's story is that whatever is inside you will eventually come out. For instance, you may have a flaw that lies dormant for years because no pressure is ever applied to squeeze that fault out of you. But then you

> Whatever is inside you will eventually come out.

are placed in a key position, and you begin to feel the heat of responsibility on you.

That's usually the golden moment you discover things about yourself that you don't like. That position of responsibility will give you new revelation about yourself — *including some things you wish you didn't have to recognize!*

Likewise, if you are given the responsibility of choosing others for positions of leadership, remember this: When you

> A position of responsibility will give you new revelation about yourself —
> *including some things you wish you didn't have to recognize!*

place a new person into a new position, it usually reveals both his good and bad traits. You see, no one is perfect. You'll never get someone who *only* comes with good traits. All human beings have areas in their lives that need hard work. So if you place a person with a serious character flaw in a position of responsibility, you can be certain that the new position will bring that flaw to the surface for all to see!

For instance, if a person has no integrity in the area of finances and you place him in charge of money, it won't take too long for him to start stealing or mismanaging money. That flaw in his character will eventually reveal itself.

Or if a person has a love of power and authority, you should be careful about giving him power or authority too quickly. If you do, you put him in a prime position for that ugly flaw to come forth! When that flaw manifests, he'll try to exercise authority he was never given. Then you'll have a *real* problem to deal with in your church, ministry, business, or organization! You'll regret the day you ever gave that person power!

Be forewarned! Even if a person has the right education and the right "look" for the job — even if he seems to have the know-how and shines more than all the others — *don't* use him until you're sure of what you're really getting. If his inward makings are compatible with yours, you'll be thrilled to have him on your team. But if his inward makings are different from yours, you'll loathe the day you ever invited him into your inner circle. *What's on the inside determines what you're really going to get!*

In the case of Saul, it's interesting that rebellion never became evident in his life until after he became king. If he was rebellious beforehand, no mention is made of it in Scripture. It seems that even Samuel wasn't aware of Saul's rebellious nature. Had Samuel known, I seriously doubt that he would have rushed so quickly to anoint Saul to be king of Israel.

Yet the Lord knew of Saul's hidden fault and still permitted Samuel to anoint him. Not only did the Lord permit it, He *ordered* this event to occur so He could demonstrate what *is* and *isn't* important to Him!

Let's look at what First Samuel 9:15-17 says about the selection of Saul to be king:

> **Now the Lord had told Samuel in his ear a day before Saul came, saying, To morrow about this time I will send thee a man out of the land of Benjamin, and thou shalt anoint him to be captain over my people Israel, that he may save my people out of the hand of the Philistines: for I have looked upon my people, because their cry is come unto me. And when Samuel saw Saul, the Lord said unto him, Behold the man whom I spake to thee of! this same shall reign over my people.**

God is all-knowing, so He already knew Saul had a fatal flaw in his character. So why did God ordain Saul to be king of Israel? If Saul was flawed *and God knew it*, why did God choose him?

Was He confused? Was He unaware of what would happen once Saul was placed in power?

No, God was very aware of the consequences of choosing Saul as king. You see, Saul was the first king Israel ever had. Before Saul came along, the Lord was Israel's only King (1 Samuel 8:7). When Israel began to seek a human lord — a ruler like the other Gentile nations had — this was their first experiment in *human leadership.*

Right from the start of this first experiment, God wanted His people to understand what *is* and what *isn't* important in His eyes in regard to the leaders He wants to use. By choosing Saul to be Israel's first king, God took His people into a spiritual classroom to teach them just that.

From this experience with Saul, Israel came to understand that God is more interested in the *heart* than in gifts, talent, education, "know-how," or looks. The heart is first priority to God. Actually, Israel should have already understood this principle. *Certainly Samuel should have!*

GOD ISN'T IMPRESSED BY AGE OR EXPERIENCE

Samuel himself was just a small boy when he was called as a prophet to all Israel. By choosing Samuel at such an early age, God had already demonstrated that He wasn't impressed by age or experience.

Eli, a priest and judge of Israel, had become slack in his spiritual responsibilities. He was so lazy in providing leadership for his own household that God called Eli's two sons, Hophni and Phineas, the "sons of Belial" or the *sons of the devil* (1 Samuel 2:12). (For more on the phrase "sons of Belial," *see* Chapter Nine in my book *Dressed To Kill*.) Because Eli was so backslidden, a time came when God no longer desired to use him.

> Because Eli was so backslidden, a time came when God no longer desired to use him.

Eli possessed a wealth of life experience. He was the chief theologian of his day. He possessed extensive leadership skills acquired through years of ruling Israel. Naturally speaking, no one was more equipped to rule than Eli. Yet even with all of Eli's years of experience, God rejected him and turned to young Samuel.

To think that a young boy could become the national prophet of Israel! Yet that is precisely what happened. God chose Samuel because his heart was right, and Eli's heart was wrong. *The heart has always been THE issue with God!*

In Job 32:6-9, Elihu said these famous words: "...I am young, and ye are very old; wherefore I was afraid, and durst not shew you mine opinion. I said, Days should speak, and multitude of years should teach wisdom. But there is a spirit in man: and the inspiration of the Almighty giveth them understanding. Great men are not always wise: neither do the aged understand judgment."

Job is the oldest book in the Bible. In reading these words of Elihu, we learn that from the beginning of time, man has wrongly assumed that age, education, and experience are the most important qualities to attain in order to be used by God. But as early as the book of Job, the Spirit of God was trying to communicate that it isn't age or experience that impresses Him. The *heart of man* is what God deems most important.

By the time God told Samuel to anoint Saul as king, it had been many decades since Samuel first stood in front of Israel and uttered God's prophetic words to the nation. An old man himself now, Samuel found himself standing before a dashing, intelligent, good-looking young man. This striking young man looked impressive — even to the prophet of God. Young Saul definitely looked like the right choice for a king.

Even as Samuel lifted his horn of oil to pour it onto the head of Saul, God was aware that a fatal flaw lay hidden in Saul's character that would one day destroy him. God *knew* Saul's kingdom wouldn't last long. But He allowed this situation to arise to demonstrate a vital truth: It isn't the *outward appearance* that impresses God, but the *heart*.

GIVE YOUR POTENTIAL LEADERS AN OPPORTUNITY TO SHOW YOU WHO THEY REALLY ARE!

When Samuel lifted that horn of oil and poured it onto the head of Saul to anoint him king of Israel, he was anointing someone he didn't know. As I said, God was using this situation to take us into a spiritual classroom and teach us a very important lesson. What lesson? Before we give someone authority, we should first *know* that person!

Years later the apostle Paul wrote, "Lay hands suddenly on no man, neither be partaker of other men's sins: keep thyself pure" (1 Timothy 5:22). It's very possible to lay hands on people too quickly — in other words, to give them the seal of our approval before we really

> Before we give someone authority, we should first *know* that person!

know them and to impart authority to them before they are ready. This is a foolish, stupid mistake that produces painful consequences, just as in the case of Saul.

If you feel God has chosen you, grab hold of that calling and pursue it with all your might and energy. But don't get frustrated if you are held back for a while by those who are in authority over you. It is wise and right for them to know you, to test you, and to be sure you are the right candidate for the job. If God has really chosen you, it won't hurt you or the call He's placed on your life to wait just a little longer. If anything, your divine call will be confirmed and reconfirmed again and again as you patiently wait for God's timing to be manifested.

As you will see in my testimony in Chapter 9, I thought I was ready for ministry long before I *was* ready. I had desire. I had ambition. I had the necessary "get up and go" to do what God had placed in my heart. But there were things in me that needed to be weeded out. If I'd gotten started before God uprooted those undesirable traits, they would have later overgrown my ministry and destroyed any fruitfulness God

> **It is an aspect of immaturity to want to do everything *right now*.**

wanted to produce through me. It is an aspect of immaturity to want to do everything *right now*.

As a seasoned leader in the Body of Christ, I want to stress this piece of advice: If *you* are the one who chooses the leadership for your church, ministry, or organization, don't move hastily! *Nothing is more important in your organization than the people you choose for its leadership.*

If you choose people who have your heart and are submitted to you and your vision, they will be a blessing. But if you choose people who have a different vision and are not in agreement with what God has put in your heart, you have invited a spiritual hurricane into your midst that has the power to destroy everything you have built. So take the time to be sure you're making the right decision!

We *all* have glitches and flaws in our character. Not one of us is perfect. Fortunately, small flaws are correctable as long we have receptive and teachable hearts.

But if a person refuses to see his need for change and is closed-hearted to suggestions made by those who love him, this is evidence of *the most serious* character flaw. From the outside, this person may look like he's just what you're looking for, but don't forget to consider the *deeper issues* of the heart.

Pastors and leaders of ministries and organizations can attest to the dreadful mistake of promoting people before they are ready. Most leaders could tell you about people they promoted into leadership too quickly — *before they really knew them.* These are the people who often betrayed their leaders, split their churches, divided their organizations, and wounded their spirits so deeply that it took a long time for those leaders to recuperate and return their lives and ministries to a state of normalcy again.

Often the hurt was unintentional. The person was simply not ready for that much power and authority. And to think that all of this could have been avoided if more time had been taken before the person was elevated to a leadership position!

Saul looked like a fine choice for a king. But there were inward, hidden problems that even he may not have been aware of. Saul had never before been in a position of authority and power over people. Therefore, perhaps even he didn't know how he'd respond to power or what kind of leader he'd be.

Put People Through a Character Test
To Find Out Who They Really Are

No car manufacturer will release a new model car to the public without first testing the weaknesses and strengths of that automobile. To test the new model, the manufacturer will have it driven as fast as it can be driven. It will be crashed into a wall. It will be driven on nails to test the strength of the tires. It will be driven over every conceivable kind of pavement and in all kinds of temperatures. Only after the car passes the final inspection will it be deemed "fit" for public usage.

To release a car without these kinds of tests would be considered irresponsible. If the manufacturer doesn't test a new model, how could he know how it will perform? How could he know whether or not it has fatal mistakes in its structure? How could he know for sure that it won't kill someone? The manufacturer is well aware that if he releases the car to the public and it falls apart or kills someone, he is the one who will be held responsible for that failure.

New automobiles are tested to protect people from being physically hurt in automobile accidents. But what about testing potential leaders to protect people from being spiritually hurt? Isn't this just as serious and an even longer-lasting danger than scrapes and bruises?

Therefore, I strongly urge you to test potential leaders before you release them to work in your church or organization. You need to know who they *really* are and how they will perform in various situations.

Inviting an untested person to be a part of your team is one of the most foolish mistakes you can make because you won't know the kind of person you're really getting. When you finally do find out, he may not perform as you expected. Then you'll have the difficult job of figuring out how to get that person off your team without hurting him or those you've placed under his authority.

Many dreadful mistakes have been made through 2,000 years of Church history simply because people were placed into leadership positions too quickly. Had time been taken and those people really been tested, it would have been clear that they were not spiritually prepared to lead. But as a result of hasty decisions and quick actions, multitudes of people have been mishandled and hurt by immature leadership.

Don't make that same mistake! Before you invite someone to be a permanent part of your team, make sure there is nothing in his character, attitude, or actions that could spiritually hurt someone along the way. Remember, you are putting these potential leaders over *people*, and nothing in the world is more valuable or precious than the people of God. You don't want to make a hasty deci-

> Many dreadful mistakes have been made through 2,000 years of Church history simply because people were placed into leadership positions too quickly.

sion that reaps terrible consequences for your church, ministry, or organization.

MAKE SURE GOD SAYS YOU'RE READY

And if you're the one whose shoulder is being tapped for a position of responsibility, put on the brakes before you shout, "*Yes!*" Take the matter to the Lord. Let Him speak to your heart to tell you whether or not you are ready.

There have been many assignments that I wanted and that others urged me to accept, but the Lord said, "No, it's not for you." Other times I knew the job was for me. But when I prayed, the Lord told me to let it pass on to another person. I was the right candidate, but there were still some traits in me that needed working on. I wasn't ready for the job yet.

As we obey God and allow His timing to work in our lives, we are never robbed of anything. Personally, I've learned to keep in step with the Holy Spirit and to allow Him to have His way in my life. As a result of waiting on His timing, I learned more that I needed to know, and I was better equipped for the job when it passed my way again. Had I taken the opportunity at that earlier moment, I probably would have made a mess of things.

If you are the one doing the selecting, it is important for you to consider two important things:

> **I've learned to keep in step with the Holy Spirit and to allow Him to have His way in my life.**

First, you must demonstrate care and love for the person you're considering to be a leader. If you put that person in leadership too fast and he "breaks down" and fails, it may be a long time before he ever attempts to do anything new again. In fact, that one failure could spiritually paralyze that person, making him afraid to ever try to do anything for God again.

Second, you must consider the health of your church, ministry, business, or organization. You don't want to put someone in a leadership position who isn't equipped to do the job because it will end up hurting the growth of the whole organization. By taking time to make sure that person is prepared, you are demonstrating the highest kind of love!

A Young Man I Chose
Who Wasn't Ready Yet

Let me tell you a story from my early ministry to demonstrate this point. Many years ago when I served as associate pastor in a large Baptist church, I noticed a young man who I believed had great leadership potential.

I was so excited about his potential that I quickly placed him in charge of an important part of our ministry. He was hesitant to accept the position and told me he felt unprepared for the job. But because of the potential I saw in the young man, I placed him in that position anyway, believing that with a little help and coaxing, he could do the job.

I pushed and shoved, trying to force this young man to be what I believed he could be. It was too early in his Christian experience for him to hold this kind of leadership position, but instead of recognizing and admitting the mistake I'd made, I just kept trying. I pushed and promoted him even more, hoping that his latent gifts would awaken and his leadership skills would come alive.

As a result of pushing this young man before he was ready, he began to feel like a miserable failure. I had given him a job that was too big and thus had unwittingly caused him to feel embarrassed and weak in front of others. But although he knew the job was too big for him, he kept trying because he didn't want to let me down.

Others in the organization loved the young man but knew he was incapable of fulfilling the responsibilities of the position I had given him. It was as if an invisible noose had been tied around the neck of the whole organization. *Unfortunately, I was the one who had tied the noose by placing an unprepared man in a pivotal place of leadership.* As sincere as I had been in making that mistake, in the final analysis my decision not only embarrassed that young man, but it slowed down the growth of the entire ministry.

This is why I say that testing someone before you place him in a leadership position is an act of love both for the organization and for the potential leader. *You protect everyone involved when you take time to know your choice is right.*

As much as that young man loved me and I loved him, the situation I had created proved to be a difficult ordeal for us both. He began to resent the ministry, and I was constantly frustrated with him because he wasn't happy doing what I'd asked him to do. But the problem wasn't his lack of desire, nor was it a question of calling. He *was* called. It was a question of *timing*.

LET GOD BE YOUR EXAMPLE

If you give people responsibility that's too big for them, they'll hate it. Their task will seem overwhelming to them, and it will be hard for them to serve with joy. That doesn't mean they *want* to be joyless. *You've just put them in something that's way over their heads, and they feel like they're drowning.* It's not fair to them, to your organization, nor to you. Everyone will be disappointed.

If you've ever been through this kind of setback because you put an unprepared person into an important position, you will recognize my advice as the voice of experience. You'll also agree that it's wise to be careful not to act too hastily. You don't need too many failures in this realm of decision-making to know you don't want to fail again!

So every time you work on selecting someone for a position of leadership, keep in mind how God deals with us personally.

- Doesn't God test us before He uses us?

- Doesn't God wait to see how we're handling current responsibilities before He gives us more responsibilities?

- Doesn't God use situations in our lives to deal with our wrong attitudes?

- Doesn't God expose our weaknesses in order to refine and make us better?

- Doesn't the Holy Spirit lovingly correct us, convict us of sin, and require us to live a crucified life?

This is how God deals with us. *So if we're smart, we'll take a lesson from Him when choosing those who will work on our team for Him!*

QUESTIONS FOR PERSONAL GROWTH OR GROUP DISCUSSION

1. Describe a challenging time in your life that was part of God's refining process to remove weaknesses in your life that might later hinder your ability to fulfill His plan for you.

2. What were the key mistakes Saul made that led to his ultimate downfall?

3. What is God's first priority when looking for someone to fill a specific role in His plans and purposes?

4. When selecting a leader, how do you avoid making a choice that you will later deeply regret?

5. Think of specific ways that God deals with you personally as He prepares you for a new season of greater responsibility in your walk with Him.

If God Chooses You, He's Already Tested You And Thinks You're Ready!

NOTES:

_____

_____

_____

_____

_____

_____

_____

_____

_____

_____

_____

_____

_____

_____

_____

_____

_____

_____

_____

_____

_____

CHAPTER 6

Why Did God Choose
A Shepherd Boy
To Be a King?

I have frequently looked at my own life and wondered why God chose *me* to do this magnificent work He has entrusted into my hands. No one is more amazed than I am when I look at the ministry God has given me.

Perhaps you've looked at yourself and asked the same question. I think anyone who is mightily used of God and has made an honest appraisal of himself occasionally looks at his life and asks, *"Why me?"* It's a natural question to pose to oneself or to God.

But there are reasons why God chooses certain people. His selection is not based on random choice. Second Chronicles 16:9 tells us that God is regularly, aggressively searching for men and women He can use: "For the eyes of the Lord run to and fro throughout the whole earth, to shew himself strong in the behalf of them whose heart is perfect toward him...."

> There are reasons why God chooses certain people. His selection is not based on random choice.

God's eyes are roaming, searching, running to and fro in the earth, seeking someone whose heart is right toward Him. The fact that God searches so *intensely* must mean that this kind of candidate is *not* found on every street!

In Ezekiel 22:30, God needed an intercessor to pray for Israel. In one of the saddest verses of the Bible, God cried, "And I sought for a man among them, that should make up the hedge, and stand in the gap before me for the land, that I should not destroy it: but I found none."

It's so hard for me to imagine that out of an entire generation, God found *none* He could use. Perhaps there were many of that generation who were praying, *"God, please use me!"* But God isn't obliged to use everyone who prays this prayer.

I am not inclined to employ all those who want a job with our ministry. If they display poor work habits and show no visible desire for excellence, I'm not interested in working with them on a professional basis. Yes, I love them, but my love for them doesn't mean I have to work with them. Those who stand by my side must have the same heart and hold the same convictions I deem to be important.

Well, as high as my standards are, God's are even higher! This is one reason I am *amazed* God chose me! I know me! I know my shortcomings better than anyone else. I know how far I am from being perfect. But when God's eyes were searching to and fro in the earth for someone whose heart was right toward Him, He saw me. Something in my heart and in my character qualified me to be used by God. That fact is a *wonder* to me.

Why Did God Choose
A Shepherd Boy To Be a King?

As I read the biographies of those who were used by God in past decades and centuries, nearly all of them stood in awe that God chose them. In one biography after the other, I read words to this effect: *"Someday when I meet Jesus face-to-face, my first question will be 'Why did You choose ME?'"*

One thing is for sure — people are not chosen by *accident.* Names were not scribbled on paper, thrown into a big brown bag, shaken up, and pulled out of the pile. If God chooses us, He does so because He sees something *inside us* that qualifies us to be a part of His team.

> If God chooses us, He does so because He sees something *inside us* that qualifies us to be a part of His team.

No story better illustrates what God seeks in people He wants to use than the story of King David. David was far too young to be a king by the world's standards. So why did God overlook other older candidates and turn to this young boy? What was *inside* David's character that caused God to choose him to be king?

David was the youngest and least experienced of all the brothers in his house, yet God passed the others by. When Samuel stood in front of David, "...the Lord said, Arise, anoint him: for this is he. Then Samuel took the horn of oil, and anointed him in the midst of his brethren: and the Spirit of the Lord came upon David from that day forward..." (1 Samuel 16:12,13).

I believe a partial answer to why God chose David may be found in First Samuel 16:18. This scripture tells us several important things about David. It reveals the qualities in his character that set him apart from others and brought him to God's attention.

First Samuel 16:18 says, "Then answered one of the servants, and said, Behold, I have seen a son of Jesse the Bethlehemite, that is cunning in playing, and a mighty valiant man, and a man of war, and prudent in matters, and a comely person, and the Lord is with him."

To understand why God chose David, I want us to take a deeper look at First Samuel 16:18. This verse tells us the kind of character David possessed *even as a child* and why God *knew* He could trust this young boy with a mighty mission.

The first clue in the verse tells us David was "cunning in playing." What kind of insight does this give us to the heart and character of David?

Far From the Big City!

David was raised in an obscure village called Bethlehem. A farmer who had seven older sons fathered him. David's family members were good, simple, down-to-earth, honest people whose lives were immersed in their rural community.

In small villages, people are naturally limited in their view of the world. Their world is the street they live on, the garden they grow, the animals they raise, and the children and grandchildren they love. The cows must be milked, the sheep sheared, the eggs collected from the chickens, the dogs and cats fed, and the garden cultivated. This is what people in the village think of and deal with day after day.

Butter is homemade. The pig and cow are slaughtered in the backyard. The house is fashioned of materials made by the father and his sons. Indoor toilets are nonexistent. There is no running water. The most basic commodities like laundry detergent and soap are handmade.

Life in the village may look quaint to an outsider. But when you take a deeper look, you'll realize why young women look old and have deep wrinkles in their faces. It is a hard, difficult life.

When our family first moved to the Soviet Union, I enjoyed looking out the window of our train compartment when we traveled back and forth from Riga to Moscow. I loved all the little log village houses with windows decorated in a special Russian "gingerbread house" style.

I saw people carrying bundles of wood and riding in carts pulled by big mules and horses. Men were cutting wood. Women were pulling buckets of water from the well. There were no telephones or modern conveniences. It looked simple, quaint, precious, and pure to my Western eyes. It seemed to me that these villagers lived their lives free from worry and care.

That illusion quickly disappeared on my first long stay in one of those cute little Russian villages. It was winter and very cold. The heat in the house came from wood burned in a wood-burning stove. But before that wood was carried into the house, it had to be chopped outside in the cold weather!

The streets of the village were nothing but brown, pudding-like mud. Denise and I tried to drive our car through that muck, but it was almost impossible. Our clothes and shoes were always filthy from the splatter of the gooey dirt. Outside on the streets, we'd watch as hundreds of sheep would push hard through the sludge, their beautiful, white wool fleeces stained a filthy, nasty deep brown.

In the house where Denise and I were staying, the lady of the house cooked bread in an oven that looked like it dated back to the last century. The house had no inside toilet, so every time Denise and I needed to go to the bathroom, we'd have to put on our boots and prepare for a walk through the mud. We'd walk past the ducks, past the cow, past the snorting, grunting pig, and past the chickens until we finally reached the outhouse.

The first time we went to this outhouse, we discovered it had no toilet — just a round hole in the ground! There was also no light in the outhouse. A matchbox sat on top of a ledge next to a candle, which was supposed to give us enough light to make sure we didn't accidentally step into the hole! Finally, there was no toilet paper — only a couple of ragged pieces of newspaper that hung on a nail on the wall. These were to serve as toilet paper!

After a few days in the village, I forgot about the word *quaint.* I saw that in many ways, village life is *horrible.* Young men look old. Young women are already aged. Life expectancy is short. Everything about life is a terrible labor. When someone dies, family members even have to go dig the hole for the burial themselves. From birth to the grave, life in the village is *difficult.*

When the family sits down to eat, the mother and sisters run from kitchen to table to bring dinner for the men and boys. Far-fetched dreams of becoming an astronaut or a bank president don't exist. These kinds of ideas aren't even entertained. Instead, Papa wants to know who forgot to lock the gate and therefore let the cow get out!

Chores begin before sunrise and last until sundown, which helps make the villagers' world very small and detached from what's happening on the other side of the globe. They don't have time to worry about the national debt. They have more important things to concentrate on. For instance, maybe when they woke up this morning, they found out someone had stolen their pig. All they can think about is the fact that they need to go out and try to get their pig back. That lost pig is the big news in their lives!

If the villagers have any free time, it's spent fixing the house, repairing the roof, plowing the garden, emptying the septic tank, or overhauling the car. Even rare times of family fun are cut short when it's time to get back home to milk the cows.

The big talk in town centers around who is getting married, who is having a baby, who is drinking too much, or whose children are doing what. Everyone knows everyone else's business. Ladies blush with embarrassment as they gossip about the boy down the street who was seen kissing a girl!

Life in the village is *simple.*

There is competition in the village, too, but not the same "dog-eat-dog" competition found in the city and business world. Local boys compete for the prettiest girls, flexing their muscles to prove who is the most masculine. Young boys compete in neighborhood contests to see who can spit the farthest. Grown men argue over whose cow gives the most milk.

Why am I making this point about life in the village? Because the place where David was raised was similar to the village described above. He lived far from the big city, and his family was busy with the daily issues of village life. I seriously doubt that anyone in that little town ever dreamed of becoming a *king*. People were probably too busy dreaming about purchasing a new *cow*!

Bethlehem was just a tiny dot on the map. It had no great concert halls or sophisticated auditoriums where people dressed in tuxedos and evening gowns came to listen to music and poetry. David's entire world revolved around his home, his sheep, his favorite pasture, his father and brothers, his musical instrument, and his relationship with God.

If David ever dreamed of becoming king, there is *no* record of it in the Bible. If he ever dreamed of playing his instrument before adoring crowds of listeners, the Bible *never* tells us. If he lay in those green pastures and dreamed about scores of future generations while writing his psalms and singing his songs, it is *not* recorded in the Bible. If David had awesome dreams about worshiping in God's temple with thousands of singers and musicians, we do *not* know it from God's Word.

But — there's something about David we *do* know! He was "cunning in playing" his musical instrument!

David had a desire to play his instrument like a *real* professional. He didn't play it for fanfare or applause. He wasn't looking to perform in some great concert hall. He played his music for himself — just because he *wanted* to do it.

While he attended his father's sheep, he reached for his instrument and sang to the stars. He sang to his flock. He sang to his God. Hour after hour after hour, he played each song again and again until he could play it without one mistake. He also wrote lyrics and expressions that came from deep within his spirit and soul.

Few shepherds in David's day knew how to write because shepherds needed no writing skills. But this boy was a masterful writer. He painstakingly learned to express on paper the deepest thoughts of his heart. David possessed an unquenchable urge to be *excellent*. This was a very remarkable quality to find in a boy who grew up in a very *un*remarkable setting!

What does this desire for excellence tell us about David? What does it tell us about why God chose David?

EXCELLENCE WILL COST YOU SOMETHING

There is a price connected to *excellence*. The highest price is the crucifixion of flesh, which would prefer to lie around rather than to accomplish something valuable in this life.

Look at a child with no parental guidance or discipline, and you'll see exactly what flesh does when it has its own way. It lies around, watches television, and eats junk food from morning to evening. If a person lets his flesh do what it wants, this is the lifestyle he will most likely adopt!

Dealing with the flesh is like chastening a child. The flesh must be controlled, corrected, and made to obey even if it wants to do otherwise. It must be told what to do and made to obey. The process is painful, but the rewards are eternal!

Hebrews 12:11 says, "Now no chastening for the present seemeth to be joyous, but grievous: nevertheless afterward it yieldeth the peaceable fruit of right-eousness unto them which are exercised thereby." Nothing is more thrilling than to see progress in your own life. The process to progress often feels long and laborious, but afterward when you can *see* and *appreciate* the results, you'll thank God you didn't bail out!

> The process to progress often feels long and laborious, but afterward when you can *see* and *appreciate* the results, you'll thank God you didn't bail out!

There have been many moments when my flesh screamed in disgust at the idea of discipline and commitment, but I knew I'd risk losing everything if I avoided the level of com-mitment God was asking of me. Refusing to deal with flesh is precisely what led to the demise of King Saul!

If you'll pay the price to become excellent, it will pay off with big dividends. So develop your gift. Cultivate your spirit. Let the Holy Spirit exercise His discipline in your life. Then in time, results will come forth! You may not see immediate, tangible results while you are training and preparing to fulfill your call, but eventually you will see the fruit of your labor.

*Why Did God Choose
A Shepherd Boy To Be a King?*

The Bible says, "A man's gift maketh room for him, and bringeth him before great men" (Proverbs 18:16). We don't know for sure that David was the most *talented* musician in the land, although that's a very real possibility. We do know, however, that because of David's discipline and commitment, he became the most *well-known* musician. His gift made room for him, just as Proverbs 18:16 says.

When evil spirits tormented Saul and he needed someone to come soothe his soul with music, whom did they call? They called *David.* The boy from the village became so well known for his musical skills that it brought him into the presence of the king.

What a story this must have been in the big city! *A child wonder!* A musical *prodigy* from the village — not taught in the professional schools of music, but self-taught out in the pastures as he tended his father's sheep!

But consider this: *What if David hadn't practiced and committed himself to excellence?*

What if he had chased birds and slept in the afternoon sun rather than strive for excellence in playing his instrument?

What if he had ignored his gifts, talents, and dreams and done nothing to develop them?

David's desire to compose and play his music with excellence reveals that he had something the other young men in the village apparently didn't have. David had *desire*.

> Desire is a person's insatiable urge, longing, appetite, craving, and yearning to stretch for something greater than he is right now.

Desire is a person's insatiable urge, longing, appetite, craving, and yearning to stretch for something greater than he is right now. Desire is what takes people higher in life, and lack of desire is what keeps them stuck in the muck of a mediocre "survival mode."

THE WAY PEOPLE LIVE REVEALS THEIR LEVEL OF DESIRE

Just recently I was driving down the street with my wife when we saw a sight that illustrated what we were talking about at that exact moment. We were discussing our concern for certain church members who reflect *no* desire for excellence in the way they live.

You see, excellence begins on the inside of you. It starts with an inward attitude, a determination to always do the best you can with what you are and with what you have.

When I see a young person who has loads of talent and potential but never combs his hair, irons his clothes, makes his bed, washes his car, or cleans up his pigpen of a home, it *deeply* disturbs me. It especially concerns me if that young person has money to improve himself but never does it because he doesn't care.

A person who never attempts to make improvements in his living conditions is not someone I want to serve alongside of me in my ministry. I know from the way he lives that he isn't a person with high standards of excellence. Likewise, an individual who is content to remain at his same level of proficiency at work, never striving for greater results, reveals a low level of desire to attain excellence.

This is probably *not* the kind of person God can trust to do big things! A person's "take-it-easy, don't-rock-the-boat, never-achieve-anything-special" attitude reveals a lack of the passion and desire needed to be a mover and shaker in life. This person could be developing his mind. He could be striving for excellence in his work. He could be reading books and developing skills of professionalism in his chosen field. Instead, he sits around in a muddle of mediocrity, satisfied with the status quo.

When we first began our work in the former Soviet Union, few opportunities existed for people to develop the kind of progressive Western ideas and habits that could help them perform their jobs more effectively and professionally. So I decided to send some of our staff members to the West to study business or ministry techniques. I believed that exposure to these new techniques would be all they needed to improve their work and level of professionalism. One after another left for the West to study the new ideas that I felt certain would help them advance in their jobs.

I soon learned that the only ones who benefited from such a trip were those who were already striving for excellence in their work. Those who aimed for excellence in the way they dressed and demonstrated an incredible desire for higher professional-ism *before* they went were the ones who improved in their work *after* they returned. On the other hand, those who demonstrated a lackadaisical attitude about their jobs and the way they dressed before they went on these trips came back completely *unchanged*.

Working in a good environment helps, but it isn't everything. If a person doesn't already have a commitment to excellence planted in his heart, you cannot put it into him. Yet that person won't achieve anything until he develops an inward desire to excel. I have personally learned through years of experience that a person who is content to live an average, run-of-the-mill, nonproductive life will never be mightily used by God.

As Denise and I discussed our desire to see our people display a greater desire for excellence, we looked out at the passing scenery. Suddenly we spotted an older lady who was a member of our church walking down the sidewalk to our right. She didn't realize we were driving along-side of her in our car. This particular pensioner was very poor, but she always looked beautiful when she came to church each week and invariably wore a smile on her face.

> A person who is content to live an average, run-of-the-mill, nonproductive life will never be mightily used by God.

Like millions of other people living in the wreckage of the former Soviet Union, this woman had lost her money, her job, and even her national identity when the Soviet Union collapsed. As a pensioner, she existed on a salary so low that I didn't know how she even survived from day to day.

She had worked her entire life in a political system that promised to take care of her when she grew old. Now she was old, and that system was gone. Her monthly pension was barely enough to buy bread and milk.

This sad situation has happened to many people in the former Soviet Union. It's heartbreaking to see so many who live in despair and have given up all hope and reason for living.

But when Denise and I saw this little woman, our hearts were thrilled! That particular day, she had put on her best dress jacket. Her hair was beautiful. Her face was prepared for the day. She was holding her head up high and walking down the street as if she were a queen!

Then Denise and I noticed that this woman wobbled as she walked. We both looked at her feet and realized her shoes were almost completely worn out and were causing her pain as she slowly strolled along. Denise exclaimed, *"Oh, Rick, her feet are hurting! We've got to get her some new shoes!"*

When I saw how this little old woman walked, it both saddened and blessed me. I was sorry her situation was so difficult that she was walking in those horrible shoes. But I was blessed that her spirit and her mental attitude were so strong that she *refused* to let life get her down.

This little woman put on the best she had in an effort to look as excellent as possible in the midst of her circumstances. Yet many other people who face much less challenging situations live pretty low lives. They sit around griping and complaining about everything. They easily give up and quit because they

> So often believers live beggarly lives simply because they have no ambition, passion, or desire to live any better.

don't have the same *desire* this woman has to keep pressing toward excellence regardless of the obstacles.

When a person first gets saved, it's understandable that his mind isn't renewed to grasp who he is in Jesus Christ. It takes time for a person's mind to become renewed to the extent that he can comprehend and pursue the higher life God wants for him.

But so often believers live beggarly lives simply because they have no ambition, passion, or desire to live any better. They maintain a self-satisfied, complacent attitude that cripples them from ever being anything more than they are right now.

I personally do not understand a person who:

- Has the ability to improve himself, but doesn't.

- Has the money to buy better clothes, but doesn't.

- Has an iron to press his clothes, but doesn't use it.

- Has a comb to comb his hair, but doesn't care how his hair looks.

- Has the opportunity to study and increase his knowledge and skills, but never cares enough to do it.

- Has been reared in a good home with good parental examples, but allows his living quarters to look like a pigpen.

If any of these points describes you, it's time to make a change!

God doesn't choose passionless people who are content to achieve nothing in life to do His work in the world. He doesn't require that a person earn a university degree in order to be used by Him. But He does look at a person's *attitude* and *desire* before He lays His hand upon him and calls him to do something historic and monumental.

I believe this principle is presented clearly in Jesus' parable about the talents. Remember, Jesus called the servant who buried his talent *unprofitable* and *good-for-nothing*.

If you know someone who is called of God and loaded with gifts and talents but who is lazy in his approach to life, let me encourage you to speak correction to this person in love. However, if he refuses to change, go ahead and turn your focus elsewhere. God will never select that person to do anything great until he becomes willing to change.

Why would God trust this kind of person with an important task when he can't even make his bed or comb his hair? Regardless of the talent or gifts this person possesses, he is eliminated by *his own lack of desire*.

When a person decides to take typing lessons, go back to school, hang wallpaper in his living room or kitchen, learn to play an instrument, join the church choir, or become an usher in his church, he reveals a lot about himself. This individual is on the road to *success*!

A willingness to learn — to try new things and develop new approaches to life — is a *requirement* for anyone who wants to succeed in life. A person can be successful, above average, *the cream of the crop*, only when he is willing to put forth the effort demanded of excellence.

> A willingness to learn — to try new things and develop new approaches to life — is a *requirement* for anyone who wants to succeed in life.

This issue of *desire* is not a second-rate issue. *It is right at the top of the list of requirements for excellence!* It's so critical to advancement in life that when the apostle Paul gave Timothy his list of character requirements for Christian leaders, the first thing he put on the list was *desire* (1 Timothy 3:1).

DAVID HAD *DESIRE*

When it came time to replace King Saul, God turned His attention to a country boy who showed more diligence than any of the men in the city. *David's desire for excellence was a part of his character.*

Desire is something you can't give to someone. It has to originate inside the person himself. If an individual doesn't possess desire, it is difficult, if not impossible, to impart it to him. David is an example of someone who had desire.

If you are the one choosing leaders in your church, ministry, business, or organization, do *not* overlook a person's desire. Is he pursuing improvement in the way he lives, where he lives, and how he dresses? Does he constantly work on developing new skills? If not, he is probably not the right person for you to choose as a part of your top team.

You don't need a passionless, desireless person running a division of your church, ministry, business, or organization. If you choose someone like that to be in charge, that division of your ministry or business will soon be *sluggish* and *nonperforming.* Even worse than that is the fact that the person you placed in charge will be *content* with the results!

Look for those who have *desire.* Search high and low for people who read books, listen to teaching tapes, and attend seminars to learn how to better perform their responsibilities and improve their skills. Choose those who strive for excellence in the way they live, where they live, and how they dress.

Remember — God's eyes run to and fro in the earth, seeking, searching, looking for those who fill the criteria He demands. So don't move too hastily as you make *your* choices. Let God be your Example. Look long and think hard. Make certain the person you select is made of the right material. Be aware that how he lives and dresses is probably an accurate indicator of the level of excellence he will bring with him to the ministry, business, or organization.

God wants to use everyone, but not everyone will be used.

What happens to people depends on what they are willing to put into themselves and their calling. If they are happy as they are, then that's all they will ever be. But if they have an inward desire to be more than they are, they will never be satisfied to remain unchanged. They will possess an appetite to get up and become something significant.

If you lack desire, I urge you to get before God and call out for Him to do a new work in your heart. Ask Him to give you a holy dissatisfaction with the status quo you're living in right now.

> Call on God to stir the embers of your heart until you burn with desire for His best in your life.

Call on God to stir the embers of your heart until you burn with desire for His best in your life. If you're not willing to do this, it really doesn't matter how gifted or talented you are — you won't be the one God chooses first.

Never forget that whatever is in a man's personal life is *exactly* what he will bring to the area of responsibility entrusted to him in the church, ministry, business, or organization. If he demonstrates no desire for excellence at home, you can be sure he won't pursue excellence in his new position either. *He cannot give what he does not have.*

Everything David did demonstrated that he had *desire.* When God saw it, He *knew* this young man had the right inward makings to become a great king.

DAVID HAD *COURAGE*

First Samuel 16:18 goes on to give us the next clue to David's character. It says that he was "a mighty valiant man."

If you haven't discovered it yet, you will soon discover that it takes great courage to do God's will. Most often God's orders don't come at a convenient moment or during an easy time. Voices of opposition — including the devil, your friends, and even your family — will tell you to back up, slow down, and reconsider your plan of action.

That's why if you're going to obey God, you need *courage.*

Courage is having the guts to do what needs to be done, regardless of the fear you may feel or the questions that remain unanswered. When you walk in courage, you have the endurance, firmness, and fortitude to take a stand and do what is right, no matter what opposition you encounter. In short, courage is having the *nerve* to do what you know God has called you to do.

> *Courage* is having the guts to do what needs to be done, regardless of the fear you may feel or the questions that remain unanswered.

Consider *Noah.* He was ordered by God to build an ark for a flood that wouldn't come for another 100 years. The laughter, scorn, and ridicule of society against his ark must have been overwhelming at times. To do what God commanded him to do, Noah had to have *courage.*

Consider *Moses.* The Red Sea lay before him while the chariots of Pharaoh pursued from behind. At that moment, Moses' flesh may have been tempted to scream out, *"GOD! What have you gotten me into?"* He had to look into the fearful faces of the Israelites, who were staring at him and asking, *"Moses, what are you going to do to get us out of this mess?"*

I am certain Moses had to push fear aside in order to lift the rod of God high into the sky above his head! To stand in that precarious place and forge ahead with God's orders, Moses had to have *courage.*

Consider *Joshua.* Joshua had to follow in the steps of Moses, who was a very hard act to follow. Moses was the greatest prophet who ever lived. He was the only person to see God and live to tell of it. He was the only person who ever spent time on the holy mountain with God. Moses received the Ten Commandments from the Lord. Moses was the instrument God used to destroy the mighty Egyptian army and to part the Red Sea. Moses was truly one of a kind.

But when Moses died, the spotlight shifted to Joshua. Now it was Joshua's turn to step into the limelight as God's new leader.

I am certain it was a terrifying sight for Joshua when he first stood before millions of Israelites and saw a sea of faces looking expectantly at him. It would have been normal for the people to question whether or not Joshua had what it took to be the kind of leader Moses had been. Joshua may have been tempted to give way to fear and take off running for some place to hide. If Joshua was going to take the job as the chief leader of this massive group of people, he needed *courage*!

In fact, Joshua needed so much courage that God *ordered* him to have *courage* three different times in Joshua chapter 1

(Joshua 1:6,7,9). Joshua had accepted the call to be Israel's leader; now he stood before the men of Israel for the first time. And what did they demand of him? *Courage!*

Hebrews 11 names others who accomplished great things for God. This chapter mentions Abel, Enoch, Noah, Abraham, Sarah, Isaac, Jacob, Joseph, Moses, and Rahab. Then it goes on to say, "And what shall I more say? for the time would fail me to tell of Gedeon, and of Barak, and of Samson, and of Jephthae; of David also, and Samuel, and of the prophets" (Hebrews 11:32,33).

Notice that David is also mentioned in this verse. David had already proven he had courage by the actions he had taken earlier in his life. Think of it! It was very bold and courageous of David at his young age to go out into the wilderness and shepherd an entire flock of sheep by himself. The very fact that David was given this kind of responsibility at such an early age tells us he was an exceptionally bold, courageous young man. *How many boys in today's world could handle this kind of responsibility?*

David had to fight a lion and a bear to protect his sheep. Even a full-grown man would be tempted to flee under similar conditions. But David took his responsibility to protect those sheep deep into his heart and soul. It was his job. He was committed to do it *regardless* of the risk or opposition he encountered.

God needed a king who would be willing to stand up for right and wrong. He sought for one who would be willing to lay his life on the line to do what was right in God's eyes. A weak man would never do. This job required someone who cared for God's people more than he cared for himself. David demonstrated *courage* to do what was right when he killed the lion and the bear. If David would do this for sheep, God knew he would do it for the Israelite people!

If you know God wants to use you but you lack courage, ask God to touch you with His power and give you a dose of His might. Remember that God didn't give you a spirit of fear, but of power, love, and a sound mind (2 Timothy 1:7).

If you lack courage, you'll be tempted to throw in the towel and quit the first time you run into a challenge. Courage will give you the inward fortitude to push those dissenting voices out of the way so you can keep going until the job is executed as the Lord wants it done.

If you are choosing people to work at your side, be careful to select people who are willing to lay their lives on the line for the message, mission, and team. Look for people who are strong enough to stand up against the opinions of the world and who can resist the voices of opposition that always come against a step of faith.

As you search for someone to help you do big things for God and take steps that will shake the foundations of hell, remember this: It's not a job for the weak-willed and opinion-driven person. You need someone who is strong and courageous enough to stand by you and walk with you into the future!

In regard to the responsibilities entrusted to him, David was all these things. From his youngest years, he had proven that he had the strength of will and character to do his job, no matter how difficult the task. David had *courage.*

DAVID HAD *PRINCIPLE*

First Samuel 16:18 gives us the next clue to David's character by telling us he was "a man of war." You see, David was governed by what he believed to be right and wrong. He was the kind of man who stood up for what was right and fought for a *principle*! No event in David's life more clearly demonstrates this than the time he fought the Philistine giant named Goliath as a teenager.

At the time, the Philistines were at war with the children of Israel. Day after day, Goliath came out of the Philistine camp to challenge and defile the name of God, yet this affront went uncontested by the men of Israel. As Goliath ranted and insulted Israel's

> David was the kind of man who stood up for what was right and fought for a *principle*!

God, the men of Israel merely quaked at the sight of the giant. Someone needed to stand up and challenge the giant, but no one came forth.

Day after day, week after week, Goliath screamed, "...I defy the armies of Israel this day; give me a man, that we may fight together" (1 Samuel 17:10).

The well-trained, well-armed men of Israel quaked at the boldness of this Philistine monster. Even King Saul, himself a mighty soldier, shuddered when he heard Goliath's threats and insults (1 Samuel 17:11). Although a sword had never been drawn and an arrow had never been shot, God's army lay paralyzed in defeat.

David's brothers had been dispatched to the front lines of battle. He wanted to join them, but due to his young age, David wasn't considered qualified to serve in the military. So his brothers went off to war, and David was sent back to the pasture to watch over his father's sheep at Bethlehem (1 Samuel 17:15).

Goliath's threats continued every morning and night for 40 days (1 Samuel 17:16). That's two challenges a day, multiplied by 40 days! The giant shouted *80* horrible, blasphemous, profane, and slanderous statements against Israel and her God. It's shocking to think that of all the well-trained and mighty warriors in Israel, not one had enough *principle* to stand up and confront those godless declarations.

One day, David's father called him from the pasture. He instructed his youngest son to take cheese and supplies to his older brothers at the front lines of battle. As David arrived at the front trench with supplies, Goliath appeared to make his daily showing. The Bible says that Goliath began to speak "according to the same words" he had been speaking twice a day, every day (1 Samuel 17:23). But for the first time, David heard those blasphemous words.

David was infuriated by the giant's bragging. He asked the soldiers standing nearby, "...What shall be done to the man that killeth this Philistine, and taketh away the reproach from Israel? for who is this uncircumcised Philistine, that he should defy the armies of the living God?" (1 Samuel 17:26).

Then later when David was brought before Saul, David told the king, "...Let no man's heart fail because of him; thy servant will go and fight with this Philistine" (1 Samuel 17:32).

David's brothers rebuked him for being too immodest. They mistook his confidence for arrogance, as is often the case with young men who are filled with the Spirit. His brothers tried to restrain him, but it was too late. David had already *heard* the words of the giant. When he *heard* those horrible, embarrassing, humiliating, insulting words against his people and his God, something inside him stood up and declared, "...Is there not a cause?" (1 Samuel 17:29).

When David heard the giant's blasphemous insults against the name of God, he could *not* stand back. Although David was younger and less experienced than the other soldiers, his *sense of principle* would not let him overlook the situation.

If no one else would be bold enough to rid the world of this monstrosity, then David would do the job. His frame of thinking would not allow him to disregard the assault that was occurring. He was driven by *principle*.

Principle is a person's inward rule. It is a conviction of what is right and wrong; a moral foundation that determines how one

> Principle is a conviction of what is right and wrong, a moral foundation that determines how one sees and responds to life.

sees and responds to life; a rock-solid belief system so ingrained into one's disposition that he cannot ignore it or deviate from it. Thus, it can be called a person's *guiding principle.*

Unfortunately, we live in a world today that has thrown *principle* to the wind. More often than not, it is a wimpish world that chooses to abandon what is right. Regretfully, even believers and spiritual leaders are often wimpish, quickly succumbing to people's opinions and other sources of outside pressures.

But when your inner belief system — *your sense of principle* — is so strong that you faithfully stand by it no matter what, you will occasionally find yourself on a collision course with the world and even with other believers who are less inclined to stand true to their convictions.

God was watching to see what David would do when he heard the giant's threats. Would he collapse under the influence of his brothers' negative opinions, or would he stand true to his convictions and challenge the giant?

David's response was *not* a surprise to God. David had already shown the kind of person he was when he faced the lion and the bear. But for both of those times, no one was around to tell him to back down or to rebuke him for being too bold. So this time he passed the *ultimate test.* He was even able to stand up to the voices of his closest family and friends. David's *principle* was stronger than all the antagonistic voices around him.

If you want God to use you in a significant way, then you must possess a strong sense of *principle*. You see, your calling and convictions *will* put you at odds with others from time to time. So if you aren't guided by an inward conviction to stand by your principles, the devil will use others to sway you from what you know to be true and right. That's why God seeks this character trait in those He wants to use — especially in this day and hour when people of principle are few and far between.

If you find yourself easily moved and swayed by others' opinions, ask God to give you the strong sense of *principle* you need to stick to your convictions and to stand up for what is right. You can be sure that if God calls you, plenty of adverse circumstances will arise to tempt you to compromise what you believe and what you are doing for God. But your inward sense of principle will keep you on track. If you don't have that, God will have a difficult time building anything meaningful through you because you lack a firm foundation on which to build.

> If you aren't guided by an inward conviction to stand by your principles, the devil will use others to sway you from what you know to be true and right.

If you are the one in charge of choosing someone, be sure to look for someone who has enough *principle* to do what's right. You see, if you're about to take your church, ministry, business, or organization in a new direction that excites everyone, it's fun and thrilling! But what if God calls you to take a direction that doesn't make people stand up and shout, *"Hooray"*? If you have chosen a fellow worker who is weak-willed or easily influenced by others' opinions, he won't be able to give you the support you need during that crucial time of transition.

Resisting a lion, a bear, and a giant were great accomplishments. These achievements, however, were meager compared to the task of leading the obstinate, rebellious children of Israel, as David would do when he became king. God saw David react *courageously* and *correctly* in the face of danger in order to stand *true* to his convictions. He knew David was a man of *principle.* This was a man He could trust with great responsibility!

DAVID WAS *RESPONSIBILE*

First Samuel 16:18 also tells us that David was "prudent in matters."

Often my ministry requires me to travel abroad to speak in churches and seminars in various parts of the world. Occasionally it means that I am absent from my church for a lengthy period of time.

But I don't fret about our Moscow church or about who will make the big decisions in my absence. Years of training and working side-by-side with my leadership staff has shown me that they know how I think and what I would do in each situation. They know me well. They have proven themselves faithful to me in many tests encountered through the years.

We've had enough experiences together for me to know they can be trusted with my church, my vision, and my ministry.

It takes commitment to survive the fires that come to test relationships. If I have a relationship with someone that has lasted through the years and has successfully overcome each obstacle along the way, I can be assured that the relationship is built on a strong foundation of trust — a foundation that will not easily crumble and collapse.

In the case of my relationship with my pastoral staff, a strong foundation has been built over the years. Therefore, I know I can trust my staff to oversee the ministry in my absence.

> It takes commitment to survive the fires that come to test relationships.

Learning to trust the people who stand by my side has been a major key to the growth and expansion of our work around the world. You see, it's impossible for me to simultaneously be at our offices in America, England, Russia, Ukraine, and Latvia. I wish I could visit each office at least once a year, but even that is becoming increasingly more difficult as my ministry responsibilities increase.

Therefore, I depend on our *Rick Renner Ministries* directors who oversee the various offices of our ministry. Our directors know Denise and me very well. They know our vision, our style of ministry, and what is and isn't important to us. These are relationships that have been tested and have survived many different fires over the years. Because of the many years of experience and commitment we have shared with these directors, I am confident of the way our ministry offices are being managed. Years of working with our directors have proven to Denise and me that these are relationships we can *trust.*

Trust is the key for the expansion of any organization. A leader can't be fearful of letting others assume leadership positions or of giving them the responsibility of overseeing whole sections of the ministry. Otherwise, his ministry will never grow.

> **Trust is the key for the expansion of any organization.**

But before I'll assign this type of top leading role to someone, I have to know that the person is called of God to work with me. I must know that the person loves me, is faithful to me, and would never deliberately violate his relationship with Denise and me. Furthermore, I must know that he or she is *trustworthy* with ministry finances and materials.

Handling money and ministry resources is a great responsibility. The money our partners sow into our ministry is precious seed. It has cost them something to sow it. I will answer to God for this money and how it is used. Therefore, giving someone authority to manage these finances is a serious issue. It isn't something Denise and I do hastily or without serious consideration. Denise and I are *responsible* for what takes place in our ministry, so we do everything we can to make sure things are being carried out in a responsible fashion.

Before you give this much responsibility to individuals, I urge you to first make sure they are with you 100 percent. You see, the only thing that proves the durability of a relationship is time and trouble. That may sound like a negative statement to you, but years of experience have taught me that most people are willing to serve when times are good. *However, what will they do when times are bad?* Will they stick around and cherish the opportunity to serve by your side even when things get tough?

> The only thing
> that proves
> the durability
> of a relationship is
> time and trouble.

So take the time to let that relationship be tested. It might slow you down a bit, but it will give you peace of mind and a surer footing as you move forward.

It is obvious that David's father trusted him. David was trustworthy enough to be put in charge of a part of his father's business, which tells me that Jesse believed David was *trustworthy* and *responsible.* This is why First Samuel 16:18 says that David was "prudent in matters."

The word "prudent" refers to *the way a person manages his mouth and his life.* Isn't it interesting that the mouth and life are connected? It is the picture of someone who is *discreet, cautious, careful, sensible, and guarded in his speech and actions.* This means David didn't run at the mouth all day long. He cautiously watched his mouth to make sure all his words counted. When he said something, he wanted to mean it.

When the Bible says David was "prudent in matters," the word "matters" refers to *work, business, or money-related matters.* This means David was punctilious when it came to work, business, or money. This quality was extremely important, especially when you consider the fact that the business he managed was *not* his own. It was his father's business. The money and resources David managed didn't belong to him either; they belonged to his father. Think how much David's father must have *trusted* him to put him in charge of so much!

Sheep were big bucks in those days. Whoever had cattle, sheep, and other kinds of livestock was rich. Even part of Abraham's riches were measured by his livestock (Genesis 13:5). To put a young boy over this kind of wealth was extraordinary! He must have been a very exceptional boy to be granted this kind of responsibility.

THE BUSINESS OF BEING A SHEPHERD BOY

When David left the house with his father's flock, he left with a packed bag because he knew he'd be gone for many days at a time. To take sheep to the best pastures, David had to lead them far from home.

Finding good pastures took time. At the end of the day when it was time to go to bed, David and his sheep were too far away to return home. So like all shepherds, David stayed out in the pasture and slept with his flock under the stars. It would be days and even weeks before he could return home again.

David was charged with the *responsibility* of making sure those sheep were fed and protected from aggressive predators such as lions, bears, and wolves. Any assault against those sheep meant he'd have to stand up and fight like a man! This was part of his *responsibility*.

Money and material resources were needed for this job. He couldn't leave home without money in his pocket, especially if he was to be gone for days at a time. So managing his father's funds was also part of David's job. He had to have a plan! What kind of supplies would he need? How much money should he take? What kind of preparations should he make in case of some type of emergency? David had to explore and answer all these questions before he took his sheep to pastures far from home.

The sheep needed to be sheared. The wool needed to be stored. If the sheep became ill, it was David's responsibility to mend them back to health. If a sheep got lost, David couldn't leave until he found it and brought it back out of harm's way. All this was part of his job!

Shepherding a large flock of sheep was a big responsibility even for a full-grown man — so think about how much responsibility this was for a young boy! The fact that David's father put him over the flock and gave him this much responsibility tells us that David had his head on straight in regard to the serious issues of work, business, and money. David was "prudent in matters."

TESTED BY TIME AND EXPERIENCE

Jesse didn't just wake up one day and say, *"David, starting today, I'm going to give you total authority over a large flock of my sheep!"*

A flock of sheep was very valuable! Those sheep were a part of Jesse's financial portfolio. They gave him status in society. They were like money in the bank! He *never* would have trusted

David with this much wealth if he hadn't already known that David was worthy of trust.

Before David got the big job, he was delegated daily chores at home and in the garden. He milked the cows, collected eggs from the chickens, and cleaned up the mess around the barnyard. Step by step, he proved his ability to handle more responsibility. He passed so many tests and did his job so well that his father eventually promoted him to watch over a whole flock of sheep!

While other boys were playing with kids their own age, David was developing and cultivating himself. Proving himself to be cautious, sensible, and careful, David became trusted with the most important details of his father's business. From way down deep inside, David lived a life that was "prudent" in every detail.

THE KEY TO RECEIVING MORE AUTHORITY, RESPONSIBILITY, AND BLESSING

> **God is watching to see how well you are handling your current responsibilities.**

God is watching to see how well you are handling your current responsibilities. If you do well, you are guaranteed to receive greater responsibilities in the future. But if you fail to correctly do the job you have now, God won't give you anything greater. In fact, the responsibilities you have now will probably be taken from you and given to someone else!

Jesus said, "For unto every one that hath shall be given, and he shall have abundance: but from him that hath not shall be taken away even that which he hath" (Matthew 25:29). So the key to receiving more responsibility is to *do* something with what you have!

God gives assignments based on a person's past and present performance. Matthew 25 makes it very clear that Jesus Christ has high standards for those who work in His Kingdom.

It is a terrible mistake to say, *"This is just a small assignment. It's not so important. Someday when the big, serious job comes along, I'll be more committed."* If that's your attitude, I guarantee you that the big job will *never* come your way.

What if David had had a lazy, do-nothing attitude? What if he had griped every time he was asked to do something? What if he had always complained that his task was too hard? What if he had grumbled all the time about being bored? Or what if he had constantly protested that his brothers had it easier than he did?

Do you think Jesse would have given David even *more* responsibility if his attitude was so stinky about the tiny, mundane tasks he'd already been given to do? Why should he be trusted with more responsibility if he wouldn't clean the barnyard with a good attitude? If David had nurtured a bad attitude, that would have meant he didn't deserve to be given more responsibility.

EVERYONE HAS A SMALL BEGINNING

You must be careful not to lament about your job being too tiny or unimportant. Zechariah 4:10 warns that we should not despise the day of small beginnings. Job 8:7 says, "Though thy beginning was small, yet thy latter end should greatly increase."

Everyone has a small beginning, so don't think you'll be the exception. Thank God for this precious time to grow, mature, and prove you are worthy of greater responsibilities. God needs to see this growth process in you. And you need to know for *yourself* that you are mature enough to move on to the next level. If the next job assignment is too big and comes too quickly, you won't have peace as you enter into it.

Learn to appreciate the stage of life you're in right now. As the apostle Paul told us, "For it is God which worketh in you both to will and to do of his good pleasure. Do all things without murmurings and disputings" (Philippians 2:13,14).

You are on *God's* schedule; He's not on *yours*. Rather than contesting your present assignment and complaining about it all the time, jump in with both feet forward! Give it everything you've got! Do the best you can!

> You are on *God's* schedule; He's not on *yours*.

Show God that your attitude is right, your heart is willing, and you desire to be faithful with the level of responsibility you've been given at this point. If you'll follow this advice, God will begin the process of promotion you've been seeking. But if you ignore this counsel, you'll be stuck in that miserable place for a long time.

So do what God has put in your hand to do! Prove yourself responsible, and you'll be given more responsibility. This was the story of young David.

DAVID HAD *DISCIPLINE*

The next clue into David's character in First Samuel 16:18 tells us that David was "a comely person."

The Hebrew word "comely" refers to *a man's handsome physique*. It is the picture of a *well-groomed, well-developed young man*.

There are many handsome young men whom we wouldn't call "well-groomed" because they have no self-discipline and they don't care about their personal appearance. It's such a pity when I see a handsome young man who looks like a bum, walking around in dirty clothes that are too big for him, his shoes untied and his hair disheveled.

What a contrast to Saul — the dashing, impressive, handsome young king! Yet King Saul thought so highly of himself that he dared to disobey the commandment of the Lord (1 Samuel 15:1-31).

DAVID WAS *SPIRITUAL*

Last but certainly not least, the Bible says that "the Lord was with David." This of course tells us that David was *spiritual*.

David had a relationship with God. When God sought for a man whose heart was after Him, where did He turn? *To David!*

Out on those hillsides in the early morning, at noon, and at night, David poured out worship to the Lord from his heart. The songs and psalms he wrote were the expressions of his spiritual life. He understood the presence and anointing of God. He longed to live in the house of the Lord and to be where God's presence was manifested.

The book of Psalms is not the shallow remarks of a carnal musician. The psalms of David are filled with prophecies that convey the heartbeat of God Himself. A stranger to God's heart could have never written such words. David writes, "...in thy presence is fulness of joy..." (Psalm 16:11). He personally knew the presence of God. He derived incredible joy from being in that holy place!

This was the central part of David's life.

As David's kingdom grew and he became a great king, his relationship with God became the driving motivation in his life. It was at the root of his being. It was a part of *his character.*

> **David understood what it meant to walk in obedience and faith, and he strove to live in that place in spite of his human frailties.**

We could go on endlessly about this point, but I think it's obvious even to the casual reader of David's psalms that he was a deeply spiritual man. He was a man of understanding. He was a man of covenant. He was a profound man of worship. David understood what it meant to walk in obedience and faith, and he strove to live in that place in spite of his human frailties.

From the life of David and the specific points listed in First Samuel 16:18, you can see that all the qualities we've discussed are issues of character, not of human talents or gifts. These are the qualities God sought when He looked for some-

> **The most important things to God are the heart and the inward makings of a man.**

one to choose to build His Kingdom. These are a few of the reasons God chose David.

So if you want to qualify to be used by God, always keep this central truth in mind — *the most important things to God are the heart and the inward makings of a man.*

QUESTIONS FOR PERSONAL GROWTH OR GROUP DISCUSSION

1. Name some of the qualities in a person's character that set him apart from the crowd and bring him to God's attention when He is searching for someone to use for His purposes.

2. Describe the price you will have to pay for excellence in your life.

3. What can you tell about a person who never tries to make improvements in his living conditions?

4. Why does God put so much importance on the qualities of *attitude* and *desire* when looking for someone to put in a position of responsibility in His Kingdom?

5. How can you determine the level of desire a person possesses to achieve God's best in any given area of his or her life?

NOTES:

_____

_____

_____

_____

_____

_____

_____

_____

_____

_____

_____

_____

_____

_____

_____

_____

_____

_____

_____

_____

_____

_____

CHAPTER 7

Exactly What Kind of People
Does God Choose
To Do His Business?

If you see yourself as weak, feeble, or unskilled, and that's your excuse for why God cannot use you, you'd better start searching for another reason! God has been calling feeble and unskilled people from the beginning of time.

Few of those whom God has called have been the "cream of the crop" according to the flesh. Again and again, God has chosen people who were ill-esteemed in the eyes of the world when He's needed a candidate or a group of people to do a job (1 Corinthians 1:27). Remember, His primary concern is *the heart*.

God has always used common people to build His Kingdom. He doesn't primarily choose famous movie stars or the royalty and nobility of the world to fulfill His plans and purposes on this earth. God's criteria are different from the criteria of the world. As Isaiah 55:8 says, "For my thoughts are not your thoughts, neither are your ways my ways, saith the Lord."

When God chose Samuel to lead the nation, Samuel was just a young boy. When God looked for someone to kill a giant, He

God has always used common people to build His Kingdom.

chose a young shepherd boy named David. When the fullness of time came and it was time to send His Son to this earth, God chose a young girl named Mary to give birth to the Savior of the world.

When it was time for Jesus to choose disciples, He didn't go to the theological institutes or seminaries of the day. Rather, Jesus chose disciples who knew more about fishing and tax-collecting than about the Scriptures. And when God searched for someone He could use to write the majority of the New Testament, He chose the apostle Paul, who once was one of the meanest Christian killers of all time!

God has always shown up in places where He wasn't expected. Just consider the location where Jesus was born — *in a lowly shepherd's stall.* This was certainly not the place anyone would have expected the King of kings to be born. Wouldn't it have been better for the King of kings to be born in a gold-gilded hall with trumpets blasting to announce His birth?

So if you have ever thought you weren't good enough for God to use, it's time for you to renew your thinking! God is looking for people no one else wants or deems valuable. When great victories are won through ordinary folks, there's no question as to who should receive the glory! As First Corinthians 1:29 says, "That no flesh should glory in his presence."

Don't discount the possibility that God may be pointing His finger at you today. The very things you think should disqualify you may actually be what makes you a *first pick* in God's mind.

Think about it. Would *you* have selected Samuel, David, Mary, Peter, or Paul? Yet these are the kind of people God chose to use in mighty and powerful ways. They may have been flawed, but they had *hearts* that qualified them for God's use.

The Old and New Testaments are filled with illustrations of people whom *God wanted,* but whom *the world rejected.* As we have seen in previous chapters, God's choice is not based on beauty or ugliness, talent or lack of talent, education or lack of education, a diploma or lack of a diploma. If a person has a *right heart* toward God, he is qualified to be used by God.

> **If a person has a *right heart* toward God, he is qualified to be used by God.**

No scripture teaches this principle more clearly than First Corinthians 1:26-28:

> **For ye see your calling, brethren, how that not many wise men after the flesh, not many mighty, not many noble, are called: but God hath chosen the foolish things of the world to confound the wise; and God hath chosen the weak things of the world to confound the things which are mighty, and base things of the world, and things which are despised, hath God chosen....**

To really comprehend the full impact of what Paul is saying, let's dig a little deeper into these words. Check to see if you fall into any of the categories that Paul lists in this passage of Scripture.

God Isn't Looking for People Who Are Intellectually Brilliant, Astute, or Smart

As Paul writes his list of those whom God *does* and *doesn't* call, he begins by stating that God *doesn't* call many who are considered "wise" by the world. The word "wise" is from the Greek word *sophos*. It refers to a person who possesses *special enlightenment* or *special insight.*

The word *sophos* was usually used to portray highly educated people, such as scientists, philosophers, doctors, teachers, and others who were considered to be the *super-intelligentsia* of the world. These belong to a class of individuals whom the world would call *clever, astute, smart,* or *intellectually brilliant.* This term was reserved only for those considered to be *super-impressive* or a *cut above* the rest of society.

But Paul says, "For ye see your calling, brethren, how that not many *wise* men after the flesh...." Paul informs us that most of the folks God calls don't fit into this category of the *super-intelligentsia.* In other words, God doesn't specialize in calling people who are *especially bright, educated, astute, smart,* or *eminently enlightened.*

I would be foolish to overlook the fact that over the years many intelligent men and women who loved God have made a great impact on the world. Paul himself was a part of this elite group before he came to Christ. Apollos, Paul's friend who later pastored the church of Corinth, also came from this intellectual "upper echelon" of society. But Paul and Apollos were not typical of the first-century Church.

It was the *sophos* who scorned and ridiculed Paul when he preached in Athens. The philosophers of Athens, the Epicureans and the Stoics, derided him and made him a laughingstock. Paul said that "not many" are called who fit into this *sophos* category. Of course, God's call is to all men, but the fact is that "not many" from this category *respond* to God's call.

Take a close look at the Early Church, and you'll see that it was primarily composed of servants, slaves, and poorer people who heard the Good News of the Gospel and believed. *It was an army of common people.*

Although there were a few elite in the Church, these were the exception rather than the rule. In fact, as we continue in First Corinthians 1:26-28, you will clearly see that God primarily specializes in calling people from a much lower class. And if you take a close look at the Church today, you'll see that God still specializes in calling common people.

Now, I'm not debasing education. People should get as much education as possible. But school-issued pieces of paper are not the criteria that impresses God and gets His attention. There have been many educated people whom God could not use. Even though they were brilliant according to the flesh, they were not worthy of being chosen because their hearts weren't right.

Educational degrees may help you get a good job and positively sway the opinion of men in your favor, but Paul makes it very clear that God is not looking for people who are *"especially bright according to the standards of the flesh."*

When God does call people who are intellectually impressive, such as Moses or the apostle Paul, He usually has to empty them *of themselves* before He can use them. When they lean on their own understanding, they are unable to accomplish what God wants. But when they lean wholly upon *God*, He is able to perform miracles through their lives.

> When God does call people who are intellectually impressive, such as Moses or the apostle Paul, He usually has to empty them *of themselves* before He can use them.

Proverbs 3:5 says, "Trust in the Lord with all thine heart; and lean not unto thine own understanding." Certainly natural knowledge and understanding are needful in the world we live in today. But if our understanding becomes the basis for our confidence rather than trust in God, it becomes a disadvantage to us. *We have to learn to use what we know, but to lean only upon the Lord and His might.*

David wrote, "Some trust in chariots, and some in horses: but we will remember the name of the Lord our God" (Psalm 20:7). The best technology of David's time was used to develop chariots. Man's greatest intellectual powers were employed to make chariots faster, stronger, and safer. In addition, horses represented natural power, strength, and might. Therefore, David was saying, *"Some trust in man's mind and his great achievements; others rely on their own natural power and might; but we will rely upon the name of the Lord."*

Perhaps you're one of those people who says, "God can't use me because I don't have enough gifts or talents. I haven't even been to college. I don't even have a Bible school degree." If you are, it's time for you to change the way you're thinking and talking. It's time for you to start seeing yourself the way God does!

In fact, if you feel *inferior* to others, remember that God regularly calls unskilled and uneducated people, such as the majority of the apostles Jesus hand-picked to serve at His side and to lay the foundation of the Church. Those apostles were fishermen, tax collectors, common people — *not* theologians.

God is looking to build a strong, powerful army. The soldiers of an army are rarely composed of the intellectually astute. Flavius Vegetius Renatus, who lived around 380 A.D., was the author of the most influential military book ever written for the Roman Empire. Look at the type of person he says makes the best soldier:

> Peasants are the most fit to carry arms.... They are simple, content with little, inured to fatigue, and prepared in some measure for military life by their continual employment in farm work, in handling the spade, digging trenches and carrying burdens.[1]

The truth is, God is looking for people who know how and are willing to pay a price — to undergo any hardship needed, to confront the power of hell, and to "dig trenches and carry burdens" until their assignment is completed as He ordered it. God doesn't necessarily need the super-intelligentsia of the world to get these jobs done. And in fact, common people are

> God is looking for people who know how and are willing to pay a price.

often God's first choice because they are already equipped to a certain degree to face the challenges and difficulties of life.

So if you want to be used by God and to serve in His army, quit complaining that you're not as smart or sharp as someone else. Where does the Bible ever say God is looking for brains? He's looking for hearts that are willing to follow Him. *If you have that kind of heart, you are exactly the kind of person God wants to use!*

GOD ISN'T LOOKING FOR POLITICIANS, STATESMEN, OR DIPLOMATS

In First Corinthians 1:26, Paul goes on to say, "For ye see your calling, brethren, how that not many wise men after the flesh, *not many mighty....*"

The word "mighty" is the Greek word *dunatoi*. It comes from the Greek word *dunamis*, which refers to *power or ability*. When it becomes the word *dunatoi*, as in this verse, it most often refers to people who have *political power or political might*. It carries the idea of a person who is *high and mighty in the world's view*.

Political power is an amazing phenomenon. Occasionally I have attended high-level functions where many of the guests or guest speakers were top bureaucrats of the European Union. I was even asked by the Latvian government to organize such an event one time. I never cease to be amazed at the feeling of "power" that exists in these kinds of meetings. When you are in the presence of people who possess "political might," a tangible atmosphere of power and influence prevails.

That power can be felt as you walk through the hallways of great governmental buildings. It can be felt when the car of a president, vice-president, king, queen, ambassador, or some other high-ranking official passes on the road with policemen riding alongside on motorcycles. It can be felt when a plane carrying dignitaries lands at the airport and the runway is immediately lined with special security forces, policemen, and local dignitaries who have come to greet the arriving guests.

In these types of situations, so often I've found myself praying, *Lord, if a person with this much power would get saved, it would have such a dramatic impact!*

Although Paul writes that "not many mighty" are called, he does *not* say "none" are called. Sergius Paulus was a political figure who responded to the call of God (Acts 13:7). Dionysius the Areopagite was a politician who took God's call to heart (Acts 17:34). However, as is true of the "wise" (mentioned in the section above, indicating those of the *super-intelligentsia*), not many from this category of the "mighty" respond to the call of God.

When the rich young ruler asked Jesus how he could receive eternal life, Jesus told him, "…If thou wilt be perfect, go and sell that thou hast, and give to the poor, and thou shalt have treasure in heaven: and come and follow me" (Matthew 19:21). Matthew 19:22 goes on to say, "But when the young man heard that saying, he went away sorrowful: for he had great possessions."

---

[1]Flavius Vegetius, *The Military Institutions of the Romans* (Westport, Connecticut: Greenwood Press Publishers, 1985), p. 14.

The rich young man received God's call, but he wasn't willing to walk away from power and prestige to fulfill that call.

Nicodemus was a politician in Israel. When he finally came to Jesus, he came secretly in the middle of the night because it would *not* have been a smart move politically for him to be seen in broad daylight at Jesus' residence (John 3:1,2). Even Nicodemus had a difficult time coming to Jesus because of the power, prestige, and position he held in the sight of people.

God's Kingdom doesn't depend on the statesmen, diplomats, bureaucrats, or politicians of the world. Certainly it would be dramatic and impacting if a famous politician came to Christ, but this rarely happens. From the beginning of the Church Age, God's people have been for the most part common folks who work regular jobs and live normal lives. These are the kind of people who respond to the message of God's Kingdom and through whom God is building His Church!

All you need is the call of God and the anointing of the Holy Spirit. With that spiritual equipment, you can move Heaven to action and push hell out of the way!

You don't have to be "high and mighty" to get things done in the Kingdom of God. All you need is the call of God and the anointing of the Holy Spirit. With that spiritual equipment, you can move Heaven to action and push hell out of the way! So if you perceive yourself to be a plain, common type of person — rejoice! *You are exactly the kind of person God wants to use!*

God Isn't Looking for 'Blue Bloods,' Aristocrats, or Cultured, High-Born People

First Corinthians 1:26 continues to say, "For ye see your calling, brethren, how that not many wise men after the flesh, not many mighty, *not many noble....*"

The word "noble" is from the Greek compound word *eugenes*. The first part of the word is the Greek prefix *eu*, which means *well* or *good*. The second part of the word is the Greek word *genes*. This is where we get the word for the *human gene.* When these two words are compounded together, it portrays people who are *well-born* or who have *excellent genes.*

In ancient Greece, the word *eugenes* meant *men of high descent,* such as sons of kings, politicians, or others from the upper crust of society. It referred to *individuals whose ancestors had been powerful, wealthy, rich, or famous.* These were high-born, blue-blooded, cultured, refined, courtly, pedigreed, aristocratic people who sustained their lofty positions in society based on their birth.

Examples of this class of people would be members of royalty, who held their exalted positions in society whether or not they personally merited those positions. They were born into the upper crust and stayed there simply because of their family name or relations.

Modern examples of *eugenes* are sons and daughters of kings and queens, who retain their royal posts simply because of the blood that runs in their veins. Other examples would be the sons and daughters of famous and beloved politicians. Although the offspring themselves may have not accomplished anything significant, their famous last name has sealed their fame and place in society. They were born with a "name" that gives them guarantees and access to privileges that are not available to common people with unknown names.

But the word *eugenes* can also refer to people who carry the seed of genius as a result of the good *genes* with which they were born. An example of this category of *eugenes* would be the family of Albert Einstein.

Some years ago, I was visiting a pastor in New York City who told me an interesting story about a visit he had with the niece of Albert Einstein. He was amazed to discover she had five earned doctorates and held several prominent positions in universities in New York City. Like her uncle Albert, she was endowed with genius in her *genes,* and it carried her all the way to the top of every field in which she became involved.

Let me give you another example of good genes. Before the Russian revolution, noble families owned the lands and controlled the territory of Russia. In 1917 when the Red Army seized power, all of Russia's rich decoration and royalty came to an abrupt end. The nobility was killed or fled to foreign countries. It looked as if history had buried them forever.

Today the communist regime is gone. A brand-new rich Russian class is emerging. People often ask, *"Who are these new super-rich Russians?"* It is interesting to note that many of them have the same family names of the old ruling class that dominated Russia before the 1917 revolution. The nobility that runs in their veins is too strong to be held down. Once again, it is taking them to the top of society.

The Russian nobility were endowed with powerful *genes.* These *genes* have been passed down to the present generation. Now the offspring of the Russian nobles are reassuming positions of power that were once occupied by their grandparents. This tendency to rule and reign is in their *genes.*

So the word *eugenes* describes both kinds of people — those born into famous families who enjoy the inherent privileges of their last name, and those who carry a streak of genius, talent, or superiority in their genes. These are the upper crust, the ruling class, the aristocracy of the world.

However, Paul says that God hasn't specialized in calling this category of people. Take a look at world history and you'll see that God *hasn't* primarily specialized in using kings, queens, royalty, politicians, scientists, philosophers, writers, movie stars, or celebrities to advance His Kingdom. From the onset of time, God has reached into the hearts of *ordinary* men and women. These are the ones who most often accomplish mighty feats through God's grace and power.

So if God isn't looking for the upper crust of society, then He must be looking to the "lower crust" — *to the ordinary, usual, regular, routine, run-of-the-mill, standard, typical kind of people.*

This means if you come from a normal, average background, you are possibly the very one God is desiring to use! Yes, He has called the rich and famous as well, but it is the regular folks who most often find themselves chosen by God to carry out His will in the earth. He specializes in using ordinary people, just like you and me.

> God specializes in using ordinary people, just like you and me.

The fact that you can't claim genius residing in your genes or nobility running in your blood isn't a strike against you either. God isn't looking for people who are geniuses or well-born, high-class blue bloods. He's looking for *anyone* who will say *yes* to His call!

So if you consider yourself to be just a regular ol' person, it's time for you to start rejoicing again! *You are exactly the kind of person God wants to use!*

THE 'MORONS' OF THE WORLD ARE GOD'S KIND OF PEOPLE!

First Corinthians 1:27 says, "But God hath chosen the *foolish things* of the world to confound the wise...."

The word "foolish" is from the Greek word *moraino*. The word "moron" also comes from this Greek word. My thesaurus gives these other synonyms for a "moron": *idiot, imbecile, halfwit, numskull, dimwit, dunce, blockhead, dope, ignoramus, lamebrain, jerk, or twerp*!

The truth is, no one is an idiot in God's view. But the world often views people whom God chooses as being *nitwits, lamebrains, and idiots*. It is worth noting that the word *moraino* was used in Paul's time to depict people whom the world scorned, made fun of, and treated with contempt.

Because much of the Early Church was comprised of servants and slaves, most of the people in the local congregations were very uneducated, uncultured, clumsy, crude, awkward, and unpolished. It wasn't that they were stupid. They had simply never been exposed to or taught about manners, culture, and refined behavior. Reared and treated as servants since birth, they'd never had a need to know these skills.

However, the early Christians' lack of polish made them look stupid in the world's eyes. In fact, the Roman Empire at first looked upon Christianity as the religion of stupid, poor people because it grew so rapidly among the lower slave classes.

Yet Paul says, "...God hath chosen the foolish things of the world to confound the wise..." (1 Corinthians 1:27). The word "confound" is the Greek word *kataishuno*. It means *to put to shame, to embarrass, to confuse, to frustrate, to baffle.* The word "wise" is again the word *sophos*, referring to those who *are naturally brilliant, intellectually sharp, or especially enlightened.* Paul is saying that God calls people whom the world considers *morons* in order to put to shame, embarrass, confuse, frustrate, and baffle those who think they're so smart!

So if anyone has ever called you an idiot — if you've ever been called a stupid imbecile, a jerk, or a twerp — it's time for you to rejoice! This makes you a candidate! *You are exactly the kind of person God wants to use!*

GOD LIKES TO USE PUNY, POWERLESS PEOPLE FOR HIS PURPOSES

First Corinthians 1:27 goes on to say, "But God hath chosen the foolish things of the world to confound the wise; and *God hath chosen the weak things of the world* to confound the things which are mighty."

The word "weak" is the Greek word *asthene.* It refers to something that is *weak, base, feeble, puny,* or *powerless.* This word *asthene* describes something that is so substandard, second-rate, low-grade, and inferior, it's almost laughable!

This makes me think of David, who was but a young boy when God called him. He was so young in age and immature in physical development that the Bible says, "And when the Philistine looked about, and saw David, he disdained him: for he was but a youth, and ruddy, and of a fair countenance" (1 Samuel 17:42). Goliath took it as a joke that David would be sent to fight with him. The giant *laughed* when he saw whom God had chosen!

The Bible tells us Goliath said, "...Am I a dog, that thou comest to me with staves? And the Philistine cursed David by his gods" (1 Samuel 17:43). Who would have ever dreamed that God would select a young, inexperienced boy like David to bring this giant down? It may have looked laughable in the eyes of the world, but this young boy who fearlessly faced Goliath in battle was the exact person God had chosen!

When Paul wrote First Corinthians, the Church was the laughingstock of the Roman Empire. Christians were viewed by the governmental powers as a weak, puny, powerless religious group. The world views the Church today in very much the same way. This perception is nothing new. It's always been this way.

The world didn't understand the incredible power God had placed both inside the Church and at her disposal. The Church may have looked lower class compared to the rich class of ruling Romans who were dressed in luxurious attire. But the Church of Jesus Christ was invested with power and authority from on High. And Christians had marching orders to take the world!

Paul warned, "...God hath chosen the weak things of the world to confound the things which are mighty." The word "confound" is again *kataishuno*, which means *to put to shame, to embarrass, to confuse, to frustrate, to baffle.* The word "mighty" is the same word *dunatoi* that's used also in verse 26, describing *people who have political power or political clout.*

When you keep in mind that it was the political arm of the Roman Empire that was trying to wipe out the Early Church, you realize this verse packs a powerful message! Paul was saying, *"God hath chosen those whom the world considers to be puny and powerless — even laughable. These are the very ones God will use to confuse, frustrate, and baffle the political powers of the world!"*

It took awhile for the Church of Jesus Christ to *put to shame* all the evil forces that had come against it. But in the end, that's what happened! The Church eventually emerged in power and changed the face of history. The common, regular, run-of-the-mill people whom God had chosen were so mighty and powerful in the Lord that they "conquered the world" for Christianity during their day!

So quit seeing yourself as someone who is substandard, second-rate, low-grade, or inferior. You are filled with the Spirit of God and have the call of God on your life. Who cares what the world thinks? Even if your gifts and talents seem small in comparison to what others possess, that doesn't mean you're eliminated from God's list of candidates. In fact, your feelings of weakness and inadequacy actually qualify you as a candidate in God's service! *You're exactly the kind of person God wants to use!*

> Quit seeing yourself as someone who is substandard, second-rate, low-grade, or inferior. You are filled with the Spirit of God and have the call of God on your life.

LOW-CLASS, LOW-DOWN, INFERIOR FOLKS ARE THE ONES GOD WANTS TO USE

First Corinthians 1:28 continues to talk to us about the *"base things* of the world."

The word "base" in Greek is the word *agenes*. It is the exact opposite of the word *eugenes* (used above, meaning *well-born* or *good genes*). The word *agenes* is made of the prefix *a* and the word *genes*. The prefix *a* means *without*, and the word *genes* is the word for *human genes*. Therefore, this word describes people of *low birth* or with *bad genes*.

This term refers to people who are just the opposite of people born in royalty and prestige. Those who are *agenes* are low-class, second-rate, common, average, run-of-the-mill people whom the world will never recognize. These are not movie stars, power brokers, bankers, high-powered educators, or people who "roll in the bucks." They are just *ordinary people* whom the world perceives as commonplace, mediocre, low-brow human beings.

This may be an accurate description of the kind of people they were *before* God called them. But after they received the nature of God and were washed in the blood of Jesus, they became so powerful in the Spirit that God used them to confound the whole world!

> **What you were in the past does not determine who you are today or who you will be in the future!**

You see, what you were in the past does not determine who you are today or who you will be in the future!

Have you been feeling ordinary and not-too-special? Well, guess what! Your "ordinariness" just qualified you to be used by God! You are *very* special. Your standing in God's eyes is extremely high. In fact, *you are exactly the kind of person God wants to use!*

REJECTED AND OVERLOOKED PEOPLE ARE CANDIDATES FOR GOD'S USE

First Corinthians 1:28 goes on to say, "And base things of the world, and *things which are despised....*"

The word "despised" is the Greek word *exoutheneo.* It means *to make light of, to despise, to treat with contempt, to disregard, to neglect.* It pictures *someone so low and detestable that he is hideous, disgusting, despicable, nauseating to the viewer.* In fact, this outcast is so low, he isn't even worth recognizing.

The force of this Greek word is very strong! It indicates that the terrible opinion described above has always been and will continue to be the prevailing opinion in the future. In other words, as long as the world lies in the grip of the enemy, the unbelieving world will not even consider believers worth mentioning, no matter how much they try to do what's right.

I relate to this word *exoutheneo* entirely! Since my family and I moved to the former Soviet Union in 1991, we have poured our whole lives into this land. We have invested our lives, monies, energies, and nearly every ounce of our strength into establishing churches, broadcasting the Word on television, and enriching the lives of people.

But time and again, I've been shocked by the editorials and newspaper articles that accuse me and our ministry of being criminals, cult leaders, a dangerous sect, and so on. One particular article deeply disturbed me. It made the statement that we had never contributed one concrete thing to anyone or anything in the nation since we had arrived in 1991. Knowing how much we have invested and how many people's lives have been completely changed by the Gospel we've preached, I was absolutely thrown for a loop by this newspaper article!

First John 5:19 explains why the world refuses to acknowledge our good deeds. It says, "And we know that we are of God, and the whole world lieth in wickedness." Another translation says, *"And we know that we are of God, and the whole world lies in the embrace of the wicked one."*

If this is the case, why should it surprise you or me if the world doesn't jump up and down about what we are doing? The Bible clearly teaches that "...the god of this world hath blinded the minds of them which believe not, lest the light of the glorious gospel of Christ, who is the image of God, should shine unto them" (2 Corinthians 4:4).

Hasn't the world always been harsh and acrimonious toward God's people? From the beginning of time, the lost world has ridiculed, made fun of, sarcastically accused, and debased the people of God. There is nothing new about this at all.

Remember that Jesus was also "despised and rejected of men" (Isaiah 53:3). You are in good company with Jesus! So if the world makes light of you or treats you with contempt — if it disregards, neglects, and overlooks you — take heart! *You are exactly the kind of person God wants to use!* He has big plans to use you as a demonstration of His almighty power to the unbelieving world!

THE RIV TRANSLATION
OF FIRST CORINTHIANS 1:26-28

Let me give you the RIV ("Renner's Interpretive Version") of First Corinthians 1:26-28:

For you see your calling, brothers, how not many of you were especially bright, educated, or enlightened according to the world's standards; not many of you were impressive; not many came from high-ranking families or from the upper crust of society. Instead, God selected people who are idiots in the world's view; in fact, the world sees them as imbeciles, jerks, real twerps. Yet God is using them to utterly confound those who seem smart in the world's eyes.

God has picked out people who are laughable, and through them He is confounding those who think they are so high and mighty. Low-class, second-rate, common, average, run-of-the-mill people – those so low that the world doesn't even think they're worth the time of day – these are the ones whom God has chosen....

Rather than complain that you're too feeble, it's time to shout for joy! Your lack of skill may be the very thing that makes God want to use you! That way, when people begin to glory over what has been achieved through your life, you can truly say, *"Believe me, if anything good has been done, it's all been through the grace of God!"*

By choosing regular folks, God has made sure that when the victory is won, everyone will know it is due to His glory and grace. As Paul said, "That, according as it is written, He that glorieth, let him glory in the Lord" (1 Corinthians 1:31).

LOOK AT WHAT YOU'VE BEEN GIVEN
IN JESUS CHRIST!

God wants to use you! He brought you into this world to accomplish something great with your life. The verses discussed above have already proven that it doesn't matter how weak, feeble, or inferior you feel. None of these deficiencies disqualifies you from being used by God.

Besides, you have been given so much through Jesus Christ! You really have no legitimate reason for failing to be an awesome success in life. You have so much going for you. In fact, you have much more going for you than you could possibly imagine!

YOU WERE BORN
BY THE POWER OF GOD

John 1:12 says, "But as many as received him, to them gave he power to become the sons of God, even to them that believe on his name." This verse reveals that you received divine power the day you became a child of God. This word "power" is the Greek word *dunamis*. It describes a power that is *explosive, dynamic, and full of phenomenal ability.* That's the kind of power that came to live inside you the day you received Jesus Christ as your Savior!

Rather than complain that you're weak and nothing special, it's time to start laying claim to what is stored up inside you!

You're full of explosive, dynamic, phenomenal ability. *You are a real dynamo!*

YOU ARE A BRAND-NEW CREATURE

Second Corinthians 5:17 says, "Therefore if any man be in Christ, he is a new creature: old things are passed away; behold, all things are become new."

This verse says you're a brand-new creature if you are in Christ Jesus. The word "new" describes *something that is brand-new*. This isn't talking about some bad thing that has been reformed into something better. It's talking about something that is *brand, spanking new*!

The word "creature" is the Greek word *ktisis*. It is the same word used to describe the creation of the world. When God created the universe, he used no existing materials or old elements to make it. Everything in creation was *newly made.*

Now that same word is used to describe what happened to you the day you got saved. *Everything about you is new!* You're not an amended, corrected, improved version of what you used to be. You are an absolutely brand-new creation! You are completely detached from the person you used to be.

Psalm 103:12 tells you how far your old ways have been removed from you: "As far as the east is from the west, so far hath he removed our transgressions from us." When Jesus Christ came into your life, He created you to be free from the past, free from the negative effects of your family, and liberated from all former hang-ups — in short, *a brand-new creature!*

So stop laying claim to your family's genetic problems, inheritable sicknesses, dysfunctional behavior, disorders, hang-ups, curses, or any other negative thing that was a part of your life before Christ. That old person no longer exists. He is *dead.* You are *brand-new.*

You Are God's
Special Workmanship

Ephesians 2:10 says, "For we are his workmanship, created in Christ Jesus unto good works, which God hath before ordained that we should walk in them."

The first of this verse says we are God's "workmanship." This comes from the Greek word *poiema.* It carries the idea of something that is *artfully created.* The Greek word for a poet, *poietes,* comes from this same word. In reference to a poet, it would denote *one who has the extraordinary ability to write or create a literary masterpiece.*

The word *poiema* tells you that when you became a child of God, God put forth His most powerful and creative effort to make you new. This word emphatically declares that once God was finished making you new, you became *a masterpiece, skillfully and artfully created in Christ Jesus.* There's nothing *cheap* about you at all! *God's creative, artistic, intelligent genius went into your making.*

It's time to stop moaning about how dumb, stupid, ugly, or untalented you "feel" compared to others. Those "feelings" are all lies. Some of that may have been true before you were born again, but none of it is true of you now that you are in Christ.

God turned you into something spectacular. That's who you are now! *So lay claim to your new identity. Adjust your thinking and talking to reflect who you really are!*

YOU HAVE GOD'S
RICHEST TREASURE INSIDE YOU

Second Corinthians 4:7 says, "But we have this treasure in earthen vessels, that the excellency of the power may be of God, and not of us."

Paul calls the indwelling presence of the Holy Spirit a "treasure." The word "treasure" comes from the Greek word *thesauros,* and it refers to *a rich treasure.* This word was used to portray *great fortune, an accumulation of tremendous wealth,* or *priceless and precious valuables beyond imagination.*

In every library, you can find a book called *Roget's Thesaurus: A Treasury of Words.* I'm sure you've heard of it. You probably even learned to use a thesaurus when you were in school. A *thesaurus* offers *a treasure, a fortune,* or *an endless wealth of synonyms.* This is the same exact usage of the Greek word *thesauros* that Paul uses to describe the indwelling Spirit.

Paul's point is that God has placed His richest treasure in us by sending the Holy Spirit to live in our hearts. What the Holy Spirit brings with Him when He comes to reside within us is fantastic. There aren't enough adjectives to describe how wonderful and rich this deposit is. *The Holy Spirit is an infinite resource of power, valuable gifts, talents, and sufficient strength to equip you and me for anything God would ever call us to do.*

Paul's sense of amazement is evident as he writes about this phenomenal treasure inside us: "But we have this treasure in earthen vessels...." The phrase "earthen vessels" is from the Greek word *ostrakinos*. The word *ostrakinos* refers to *earthenware made from the basest, lowest quality of clay.* Because this earthenware was made of low-quality materials, it was easily broken.

> The Holy Spirit is an infinite resource of power, valuable gifts, talents, and sufficient strength to equip you and me for anything God would ever call us to do.

Remember, Paul was writing to the Corinthians. The city of Corinth was famous worldwide for its pottery production. Corinthian pottery was beautifully covered with decorative hand-painting. This cosmetic treatment made it appealing to the eye, but underneath that beautiful paint was still a poorly made vessel. It was cheap to buy, easily broken, and inexpensive to replace.

One would never place a seriously rich treasure inside this type of earthenware for safekeeping. Instead, trained guards kept watch over fortress-like vaults — rooms that were specially built to protect priceless treasure from thieves and intruders.

I have visited these treasure rooms in castles and fortresses all over Europe and Russia. I never cease to be amazed at the treasure rooms themselves. These rooms were magnificently built to contain treasure. Fortified with thick stone walls and doors made of iron, the treasure rooms were placed so deep inside a fortress that they were nearly impossible to penetrate.

Similarly, the treasures of Egypt were hidden away in ornate, secret passageways. The interiors of these passageways were decorated with gold, and the walls were inlaid with precious and semiprecious stones. All this fantastic decoration was just for the vault that contained the wealth, which was hidden away in the deeper parts of the chamber. It was the Egyptian custom to store great treasures in fabulous hiding places.

But when God looked for a place to hold *His* Treasure — *the Holy Spirit* — He didn't look for a vault or secret chamber made of gold, silver, or precious stones. Instead, He placed His Spirit in fragile, short-lived vessels made of human flesh. *He chose you and me!* We are the *earthenware* God has chosen to hold His Spirit in this world. *We are the chambers for the treasure of the Holy Spirit!*

The human body is a wonder created by God that demands our highest respect. Mankind doesn't have the ability to duplicate this fantastic creation. However, we must never forget that, magnificent as the human body is, it was created from dust. It returns to the dust of the earth again when the spirit of man departs and the body dies.

From dust we are taken, and to dust we return. So as we read what Paul wrote about the Holy Spirit dwelling inside us, we can sense his amazement that God would place such a precious treasure inside such short-lived, dust-made vessels.

When the Holy Spirit releases His anointing and power through us, our human flesh becomes energized. Difficult tasks become easy. At moments like these, we feel almost like Hercules as God's power flows through us and we temporarily lose touch with the limitations of our humanity.

For instance, when the Spirit of God came upon Elijah in the Old Testament, he was able to outrun the king's chariots. And just think about what happened when the Holy Spirit came upon Samson. He was able to kill thousands of Philistines with the jaw of a donkey. He even pulled down an entire pagan temple fashioned of heavy stones!

The Holy Spirit releases a special anointing on special occasions that raises us above the level of our normal flesh-bound limitations. However, such spectacular manifestations of God's power don't happen all the time. Although the Spirit dwells within us on a permanent basis, the flow of His supernatural power through us to accomplish incredible feats is *not* permanent. Every time God supernaturally manifests His power through us, we have to come back down to a more "normal" level where we learn to walk with God by faith and in love, just as other people do.

Perhaps one day in the future, the Church will move into a realm of continually manifested supernatural power. But so far, no one has walked in this level of uninterrupted supernatural power except Jesus Christ Himself.

While that power is flowing, you may feel as if you're a one-man show who can do everything needed in a given situation. But just wait a little while longer, and the feelings of your

> **Even though the incredible power of God lives inside your spirit, you still need others to help you carry that vision all the way to fulfillment.**

humanity will take over. Soon you'll start calling for a team to assist you in fulfilling your God-assigned task! Even though the incredible power of God lives inside your spirit, you still need others to help you carry that vision all the way to fulfillment.

YOU ARE SEALED AND GUARANTEED BY GOD'S SPIRIT

Ephesians. 1:13 says, "...in whom also after that ye believed, ye were sealed with that holy Spirit of promise." Notice this verse says you were "...*sealed* with that holy Spirit of promise." The word "sealed" is the Greek word *sphragidzo*. This is extremely important.

Seals were used in New Testament times to guarantee that the contents of a package were *complete* and *not defective*. Such a seal would only be placed on a package if the product had been *thoroughly examined and inspected* to make sure it was *fully intact and complete*. If it were broken, defective, or faulty, the guarantor would not put his seal upon it. *The seal was proof that the product was impeccable.*

Such seals were also put on parcels before being mailed to their final destination. Parcels bearing such "seals" were usually sent by extremely wealthy individuals. These seals, which bore the insignia of a particular wealthy or famous person, meant that this package was to be *treated with the utmost tender care.*

To seal such a package, the sender poured hot wax onto the flap of the envelope or the string that bound the box. Afterwards, he pressed his insignia into the wax, leaving a visible, distinctive mark. This insignia alerted everyone that the package was the possession of a wealthy or powerful person. Therefore, the "seal" guaranteed that the package would make it to its final destination.

Well, the Bible says *you* are "sealed" with the Holy Spirit of promise. This means there is *nothing incomplete or defective* about you. When God made you new, the last thing He did was check you out, thoroughly examining and inspecting you *before* placing His final seal of approval on your heart.

If you're saved, you're sealed with the Holy Spirit. That means your contents are God-approved!

So quit treating yourself as if you are "damaged goods." You're *not* damaged! You are approved, endorsed, recognized, affirmed, sanctified, and notarized by the Spirit of God. You have the seal of God's approval, so start acting as if you're special. God thinks you are *very* special!

The "seal of the Holy Spirit" is also the guarantee that you're going to make it to your final destination. So when the devil speaks to your mind or your flesh screams that you're *not* going to make it, rebuke those lies and point to the seal God has placed on your life.

God is the One who inspected and packaged you. He also put His guarantee on you to ensure that you're delivered to His ordained destination for your life. That means you should never

> God put His guarantee on you to ensure that you're delivered to His ordained destination for your life.

complain that you're not going to make it. *Of course you're going to make it. God will see to it!*

When demons and angels see the seal of God on your life, they know they are not to mess around with that package. *You're a special package, to be treated with special care.* Angels watch over you and guard your safe passage from one place to the next. Evil forces may attempt to delay the timing of your arrival, *but the seal of God in your heart guarantees that you'll get there.*

YOU HAVE THE ARMOR OF GOD
TO DEFEND YOU

Ephesians 6:12-18 describes the spiritual armor God has given so you can successfully wage warfare against the devil and his demons. Ephesians 6:11 says, "Put on the whole armour of God, that ye may be able to stand against the wiles of the devil."

The phrase "whole armour" is taken from the Greek word *panoplia,* and it refers to a Roman soldier who is fully dressed in his armor from head to toe. Since this is the example the apostle Paul puts before us, we must consider the full dress, or *panoplia,* of the Roman soldier (for a more detailed discussion, *see* my book *Dressed To Kill*).

The Roman soldier of New Testament times wore armor that was both offensive and defensive. When a Roman soldier was dressed in this full body equipment, he literally became a weapon that was dressed to kill. It was nearly impossible to stand against a soldier dressed in such clothing.

The Bible promises spiritual armor to every believer who abides in his relationship with Jesus Christ. As long as that believer continues to draw from the Spirit of God, he or she will be supernaturally clothed with power from on High and supernaturally equipped with "the armour of righteousness on the right hand and on the left" (2 Corinthians 6:7).

Satan is unable to successfully oppose any believer dressed in this heavenly equipment. Believers who use these heavenly armaments are equipped to withstand the forces of hell. Dressed in the armor of God, they can drive demons out of the way and press into the territory God has promised to give them.

You Have Jesus
As Your Personal Intercessor

Hebrews 4:14 says, "Seeing then that we have a great high priest, that is passed into the heavens, Jesus the Son of God, let us hold fast our profession."

According to this verse, Jesus lives forever to make intercession on your behalf. This means there is never a moment when Jesus Himself is not interceding for your victory and success. The devil may try to tell you that you're standing all alone in your walk of faith; he may tempt you to believe that no one is aware of the difficulties you are facing as you pursue God's call on your life. But that isn't true. Jesus is aware of everything you face, and He's making intercession for you *right now*.

No one wants you to succeed more than Jesus Himself. He knows the challenges you will face as you pursue what He has put into your heart. He knows the devil will try to abort your dream. He knows you will face moments when you are physically tired and mentally exhausted. Jesus understands every single emotion and temptation you will ever face. Remember, He also faced temptation during His own walk of faith.

> There is never a moment when Jesus Himself is not interceding for your victory and success.

Hebrews 4:15,16 says, "For we have not an high priest which cannot be touched with the feeling of our infirmities; but was in all points tempted like as we are, yet without sin. Let us therefore come boldly unto the throne of grace, that we may obtain mercy, and find grace to help in time of need."

As our High Priest, Jesus understands everything you and I will ever face. He can be touched with the feelings of our infirmities. As a father has pity on his children, so the Lord has pity on us (Psalm 103:13). He knows our frame and that we are made of dust (Psalm 103:14).

Because Jesus is aware of these infirmities and limitations, He has assumed the role as our Intercessor. As our personal Advocate, Counselor, or Attorney, He pleads our case before the Father and lays claim to our lawful rights.

You need never feel that you are alone in your journey of faith. Jesus is right there with you, praying and interceding on behalf of you, your calling, and the needs you may be facing right now.

You Have God on Your Side

Romans 8:31,35 says, "What shall we then say to these things? If God be for us, who can be against us?... Who shall separate us from the love of Christ? shall tribulation, or distress, or persecution, or famine, or nakedness, or peril, or sword?"

God is on your side! He's the One who called you, and He's the One who will empower you to fulfill your life assignment. Always keep this in mind: Regardless of the obstacles and the opposition that come against you, *nothing* — including tribulation, distress, persecution, famine, nakedness, peril, or sword — can separate you from the love of Christ and from His desire to make you a conqueror in life!

> God is the One who called you, and He's the One who will empower you to fulfill your life assignment.

Romans 8:37 says, "Nay, in all these things we are more than conquerors through him that loved us." No matter how much the enemy tries to lie to you or tell you how unworthy you are to be used by God, you are destined to win the battle and achieve your God-given goals!

Romans 8:38,39 says, "For I am persuaded, that neither death, nor life, nor angels, nor principalities, nor powers, nor things present, nor things to come, nor height, nor depth, nor any other creature, shall be able to separate us from the love of God, which is in Christ Jesus our Lord."

The apostle Paul faced death, attacks from principalities and powers, and many other forms of opposition that would have crippled a normal man. But because Paul had learned the secret of depending on the power of the Holy Spirit, none of these things ever permanently affected him or stopped him from accomplishing what God put in his heart to do.

So as *you* begin the pursuit of fulfilling God's call on your life, never forget that God is your Partner and He's on your side. Let that knowledge encourage you to *never* give up and quit. You don't want to end up in the same category as the *wicked, slothful,* and *unprofitable* servant in the parable of the talents (Matthew 25:26,30)!

Hang tight! Hold on! Keep your focus on the finish line! Don't let the devil or your flesh talk you out of doing the will of God. *Everything depends on your obedience!*

IF YOU DON'T CRUCIFY YOUR FLESH, YOUR FLESH WILL CRUCIFY YOU!

We've looked at the criteria God uses when selecting people to use in the work of His Kingdom. But let me speak to you a little more about what will occur if you allow your flesh to seize control of your life.

Flesh is flesh. It's no different than it was almost 2,000 years ago when the apostle Paul told us it needed to be crucified. *It still needs to be crucified.* It must be dealt with on a daily basis if you are going to keep it under control.

I promise you, if you don't crucify your flesh, your flesh will crucify you! If you don't take charge of your flesh, your flesh will take charge of you!

Left unchecked, your flesh will run you over, take charge of your emotions, and promote laziness. It will tell you that you've done too much; you've already done more than anyone else; you don't need to do anymore; and you're not as appreciated as you ought to be. Your flesh will advise you to take it easy, kick back, cut yourself slack. It will scream that if anyone deserves to do nothing for a while, it's *you*.

Rest is normal and needed, but flesh tries to take everything to an *extreme*. If you allow your flesh to control you, it will carry you into a state of laziness that sedates your whole outlook and destroys your productivity. You'll lose your joy, hope, victory — even your very reason for living. In the end, you'll become weak, powerless, and devoid of the desire or energy to pursue *anything*, let alone the high calling God has for your life.

Be forewarned! Flesh will take you down a road of degeneration. You'll begin to gain weight, look sloppy, and court financial disaster. If you go the way of the flesh, you may as well go straight to the store and buy yourself a television set and a comfortable couch, because that's where you'll end up. You'll sit around flipping the remote control and wasting your precious life away. That's exactly where your flesh will take you if you don't take charge of it.

> **If you allow your flesh to control you, it will carry you into a state of laziness that sedates your whole outlook and destroys your productivity.**

The picture I've just painted for you may not be a pretty one, but it's a prophetic vision of your future if you don't decide to tell your flesh to shut up and get back on the cross!

MOANING AND GROANING DOESN'T CHANGE ANYTHING

Oh, how the flesh loves to complain and wallow! As a matter of fact, if you allow it to do so, your flesh will moan and groan all day long. This is usually just an attempt to get attention so others will feel sorry for you and come into agreement with your flesh that your dilemma is too hard to beat! *Lies, lies, lies! Excuses, excuses, excuses!*

When your flesh rises up and tempts you to be slothful about your dream, your business, or your relationship with God, *what should you do?* Or when your flesh coaxes you into believing you are too poor, too stupid, too ugly, too uninteresting, or too run-of-the-mill to be used by God, *how should you respond?*

Should you cry and complain that you're just not as talented as others? Grieve that you're not as skinny as someone else? Whimper that you weren't born into a more prestigious family? Should you lament that you were never able to finish your education? Will that put a degree on your wall?

No, moaning and groaning changes nothing! As a matter of fact, moaning and groaning usually only prolongs defeat, agony, and despair. It's *unhealthy* and *fruitless*. It's a wretched, contemptible, sordid attitude that eventually produces an *inferiority complex* and aborts your God-given potential.

Grunting, groaning, whooping, and wailing isn't going to change a single thing in your life. It's time to tell the flesh to shut its loud mouth! Then grab hold of the power of God to change *you* and the way *you* are thinking. As long as you allow that rank, stinking flesh to produce a "poor me" mentality, you're not going to make any significant contribution to the world. And that's such a pity because *God wants to use you*!

RECKON YOUR FLESH TO BE DEAD TO SIN AND ALIVE TO GOD

The New Testament tells us that we must "mortify" the flesh. The apostle Paul wrote, "*Mortify* therefore your members which are upon the earth..." (Colossians 3:5). In Romans 6:11, Paul wrote that we are to reckon ourselves as *dead* unto sin. The words "mortify" and "dead" both come from the same Greek word *nekros*, which is the word for a *human corpse*.

When I served as an assistant pastor in the Southern Baptist Church, the senior pastor wanted to teach me how to conduct funerals, so he took me to funeral after funeral. He wanted me to learn how to conduct myself in delicate and difficult situations.

One funeral I attended was an unforgettable experience. I can vividly see it even now as I write about it. It was a funeral conducted for an unsaved family whose son had tragically died in an accident. The sorrow and remorse in that room was so thick, it could almost be cut with a knife.

Nothing is sadder than a funeral with a family of unbelievers. They have no faith and no hope. When they lose a loved one, it is truly a catastrophe because their lack of hope overwhelms them. Even worse than attending such a funeral is to be called upon to *conduct* it!

I watched as the mother approached the casket to tell her son good-bye one last time. She was so overwhelmed with grief that she crawled *into* the casket! She clutched and held tightly to her son's dead body, pleading, *"Talk to me! Talk to me! Don't leave me like this!"* Funeral-home workers had to pull her out of the coffin and escort her to the limousine that awaited to take her and the rest of the family to the cemetery for the burial.

That early experience is etched forever in my memory. I've never forgotten that pitiful sight as the mother gripped that dead body in her arms and begged it to speak to her one last time. But that body was *not* going to talk to her. It was *dead*.

The empty shell that lay in that casket was the deceased, expired, finished shadow of a young man who had once lived but was now gone. There was no heartbeat, no breath in his lungs, no pulse to feel in his wrists. The clock had quit running for that man's life, and there was no turning back the clock to make it start ticking again. It was a "done deal." This man's life had expired. His body was *mortified*.

Well, your flesh needs to be *mortified* in the same way. Deal with your flesh and tell it to shut up. Don't allow it to lord itself over you any longer, always making excuses for why it can't be used by God. You don't have to let your flesh and emotions give you the run-around. You can make the decision to "...yield yourselves unto God, as those that are alive from the dead, and your members as instruments of righteousness unto God" (Romans 6:13).

Instead of focusing on what you *can't* do, it's time to start thinking of what you *can* do when you become yielded to the Spirit of God. When your body, mind, and emotions are submitted to the Holy Spirit, you cease to be a slave to them. Instead, your body and emotions become *your* servant — instruments of righteousness to help you achieve what God put in your heart.

> Instead of focusing on what you *can't* do, it's time to start thinking of what you *can* do when you become yielded to the Spirit of God.

The only way you and I will ever accomplish what we were born to do is to put the lies of the enemy aside; tell our lazy, complaining flesh to keep its mouth shut; take charge of our emotions; and yield ourselves as instruments unto God. Then as we start speaking the truth of God's Word, drawing upon His power that works in us and through us to do His will, we'll start seeing supernatural results and achievements!

God has something awesome for you to do. Absolutely *nothing* can keep you from doing what He has put in your heart — not your education, status in society, political affiliation, or physical appearance. None of these factors will have any impact on God's call on your life.

The one factor that does impact God's ability to choose you is your own obedience to Him. Your heart must be willing. You must take authority over the flesh that would take you down a lazy path. And you must yield your body to God's Spirit as an instrument of righteousness. That's when you'll find yourself on the path that leads to being used by God!

QUESTIONS FOR PERSONAL GROWTH OR GROUP DISCUSSION

1. Why are the people whom the world deems valuable seldom used by God to fulfill His purposes?

2. What are two of the primary things you need in order to get things done in the Kingdom of God?

3. What negative things have you said or thought about yourself in times past that made you doubt that God could use you?

4. What steps can you take to change your way of thinking about yourself so that you begin to see yourself as *God* sees you?

5. Write down at least three scriptures that proclaim how God sees you in Christ Jesus. Then meditate on these scriptures today, and confess them with your mouth until you actually *believe* them in your heart!

Say Yes!

NOTES:

_____

_____

_____

_____

_____

_____

_____

_____

_____

_____

_____

_____

_____

_____

_____

_____

_____

_____

_____

_____

_____

_____

_____

CHAPTER 8

Although Chosen by God, Paul's Character Had To Be Changed Before God Could Use Him

We've already talked about the many difficult challenges the apostle Paul faced as he fulfilled his divine call to the ministry. But in First Thessalonians 2:4, Paul tells us that *before* God used him in public ministry, God *first* put him through the fires of testing to purify his character of impurities that would have later weakened his ministry. This testing period was *essential* if Paul was to have a strong, enduring ministry.

You see, Paul was mightily blessed with gifts and talents. Leadership and genius were in his genes. This was evident when Paul (who was called Saul at the time) was still a relatively young man and emerged on the scene as one of Israel's foremost leaders. His God-given abilities were recognized and operating long *before* he came to Christ.

After Paul was born again, God used his extraordinary abilities to advance the Gospel, establish the Church, and write more than half the books of the New Testament. But before God could use these gifts and talents, Paul's character first had to be *changed* by the Spirit of God. Once the Holy Spirit had tempered Paul's character, even greater gifts and anointing began to function in his life.

When I talk about the need for a person's character to be changed, I am not discounting the powerful effects of the new birth. When God's nature comes into a human spirit at the time of salvation, it brings such a force of resurrection power that spiritual death is forced out and replaced by the life of God. The effect of the new birth on a person's life is beyond one's ability to describe in words.

But it is *the human spirit* that is reborn at the moment of salvation, *not* the body, mind, or emotions. The mind, soul, and body must be subjugated to that new inner life if it is to reflect the changes that have taken place on the inside.

If a person does nothing to bring his body, mind, and emotions into subjection to his recreated spirit, these aspects of his being will remain as they are, even though his inward man has changed. Only when he submits his body, mind, and emotions to the authority of the Holy Spirit and of God's Word will he experience change in the physical and soulish realms. This is how it works with everyone who makes Jesus the Lord of his or her life.

To undo wrong thinking takes time — often *a lot* of time. Changing a person's emotional makeup is no small task. It requires a major overhaul and a tremendous work of the Holy Spirit. Paul was a man who had lived as an unsaved man for many years. Although he was now reborn by the Spirit of God, he needed time to renew and retrain his soul to think in line with God's Word, just as you and I do.

PAUL'S OWN NEED

To Be 'Purged by Fire'

Naturally speaking, Paul was a talented and gifted man. Before getting saved, he had been a politician, a lawyer, a member of the Sanhedrin, and part of the Sanhedrin forces sent with special authority to imprison and kill Christians (Acts 9:2). But he'd also been an angry and violent man. In First Timothy 1:13, Paul described his former self as "a blasphemer, and a persecutor, and injurious."

The word "blasphemer" means *to ridicule, to speak ugly, to speak of with no respect.* It is particularly used to demonstrate the attitude of a man who has no respect for the things of God. Paul was raised as a strictly religious Jew. But the fact that he would use this word "blasphemer" to describe himself prior to his salvation implies that although his outward service to God was impeccable, his heart was far from God.

Paul also said he was a "persecutor." We have already established that he had special authority from the Sanhedrin to imprison and kill Christians. But most people don't understand that Paul not only killed Christians for religious reasons; he persecuted and killed them for *enjoyment.*

The third word Paul used was "injurious," which is the Greek word *hubristes.* This is the word for a *sadist* or *one who maliciously mistreats, publicly ridicules, and physically abuses someone for the sake of his own enjoyment.* We'd say this kind of person is *sick.*

So the word "injurious" indicates *a very twisted sort of perversion.* Yet this is the very word Paul used to describe his own frame of mind before his conversion.

This means that when whips slashed across believers' backs, Paul *enjoyed* it. When they screamed out in pain, it gave him *pleasure.* When he saw their blood splatter, it gave him a *thrill.* No wonder he wrote, "...Christ Jesus came into the world to save sinners; *of whom I am chief*" (1 Timothy 1:15). Many years later when he wrote this verse, he was still remorseful for the terrible things he had done to brothers and sisters in Christ and amazed at God's grace to save and redeem him.

What Paul had done to Christians was so well known that when he first came to Christ and began attending church meetings, it was hard for the early Christians to believe he was really saved (Acts 9:26). Yet Paul's conversion was *miraculous.* A light shone out of Heaven, and an invisible force slapped him to the ground. Then a voice spoke from Heaven.

Paul was temporarily blinded by the great glory he beheld on the road to Damascus. But after three days of blindness, he was healed, filled with the Holy Spirit, and baptized in water. Prophecies were spoken over him, revealing that he would have a ministry to the nations and even to kings, as well as to the children of Israel. *Paul knew he was chosen by God!*

A few days after getting saved, Paul began to preach in the synagogues in Damascus. Then he turned his attention to *Jerusalem.* He was off to tell the church leadership of Jerusalem his story and to join the ranks of the apostles! Acts 9:26 tells us he actually tried to "join" himself to the disciples, the leaders in Jerusalem.

Imagine a new believer trying to become a leading disciple overnight! But because Paul had been "big" in the world as an unsaved man, he thought his former fame would give him special status in the Church as well. *He was about to discover that who a person is in the world does not affect who he is in the Church!* This would prove to be a long, hard lesson for a proud man with a strong will to learn.

Acting independently and without the approval of church leadership, Paul began to dispute with the Grecians about Jesus, causing such a riot that the Grecians began to plot how to kill him. When the leadership in the Jerusalem church heard what was happening, they "sent him forth to Tarsus" (Acts 9:30). In other words, they put Paul on a boat and shipped him out of town!

Once Paul had left town, Acts 9:31 says, "Then had the churches rest throughout all Judaea and Galilee and Samaria...." The leadership had to get Paul out of town so the believers could get some rest! This Jewish believer was causing a disturbance everywhere he went!

After Tarsus, Paul went out into the wilderness of Arabia (Galatians 1:17), where for three years he was supernaturally taught by Jesus Christ. Paul later wrote, "But I certify you, brethren, that the gospel which was preached of me is not after man. For I neither received it of man, neither was I taught it, but by the revelation of Jesus Christ" (Galatians 1:11,12).

During the three years Paul resided in the wilderness of Arabia, he experienced a divine encounter similar to Moses' experience on Mount Sinai. As Moses had seen and talked with God, now Paul was supernaturally taught by Jesus Himself. It was a vision that lasted throughout the entire term of those years in Arabia. Jesus Himself taught Paul the major doctrines that he'd later write down in his epistles to the churches.

Then suddenly the vision ended.

It was time for Paul to leave the wilderness and start his ministry — or so he thought. Through a series of complex events, Barnabas brought him to the city of Antioch, a great spiritual center for the Church. Yet rather than welcoming Paul as a great celebrity, it seems that the church of Antioch simply absorbed him as another brother. No fanfare. No applause. This was the beginning of the fire that God sent to *test* his character and prepare him for the future.

The following years of Paul's life are silent years. Revival was erupting all over the Roman Empire. Churches were being birthed. Great evangelical crusades were being held in various places. Between Acts 9 and Acts 13, no mention is made of Paul's preaching, nor of any crusades where he participated, nor of his teaching or apostolic ministry. Acts 12 does record a missionary trip in which Paul participated. But besides this trip, it seems that Paul didn't assume any primary leadership position in the Antioch church for some time.

During that time of waiting, it must have been difficult for Paul as he sat and listened to other speakers. He could speak Greek better than any of them. He was educated in the deepest

Hebrew theological thought. He was more cultured than all of them combined. And he was the only one who could claim that he had been personally taught by Jesus Christ for three years!

It must have been a very difficult experience for Paul as he waited for his time of ministry to come. *But his ministry didn't come for a long, long time.*

PUT THROUGH THE FIRE

Paul later told the Thessalonians about this time in his life. He said, "But as we were allowed of God to be put in trust with the gospel, even so we speak; not as pleasing men, but God, which trieth our hearts" (1 Thessalonians 2:4).

This verse is packed with powerful truths about being tried and purified by the fire of God! The word "allowed" is the Greek word *dokimadzo*. It describes *the process used to determine the purity and strength of metal.*

In order for metal to be made pure and strong, it had to be put through several degrees of fire. This process exposed all the impurities that were not visible to the eye. As the first degree of fire brought the impurities to the surface, the refiner scraped them off and threw them away. Then the fire was turned up again.

Once the second, more intense blaze was ready, the metal was reinserted to be tried a *second time.* When the impurities not revealed by the first fire came to the top, the refiner poked his instrument into the molten metal to scrape them off and discard them.

Now the molten metal looked pure to the eye. However, two refinements by fire alone would never be sufficient to remove all the hidden imperfections. Therefore, the intensity of the fire was increased a *third time.*

This time the fire was made blazing white-hot so all the remaining ugly impurities would come rising to the top. The refiner scraped away the last dross and permanently freed the metal of defects that would weaken it. This entire process of purifying by fire is encompassed in the Greek word *dokimadzo,* or "allowed," used in First Thessalonians 2:4.

Paul is giving us his own personal testimony of what he felt and experienced as he waited all those years for his ministry to begin. According to Paul, it was *dokimadzo,* a very trying and fiery experience.

It must have frustrated Paul to know he could preach better than those whose teaching he sat under, yet his own ministry wasn't being especially spotlighted. He could have taught the Word more accurately, yet he wasn't the one being invited to speak. He could speak grammatically better than the speakers and ministers who came to the Antioch church, yet he was supposed to sit and receive from them just like everyone else.

At times it must have been difficult for Paul to submit and wait. It must have felt as if he were being put through the first, second, or even third degree of fire during this season of testing.

This was the hand of God reaching into those areas of Paul's character and soul that needed to be changed. Although he was mightily gifted and filled with revelation, *his character had not yet attained the level of his revelation.* Receiving divine insight was enjoyable to Paul, but being changed so that revelation could operate in his life was *painful.* The fire of God exposed those defects of which he was unaware in his life.

I think it's safe to assume that during those years of waiting, any *wrong attitudes* in Paul came to the surface. Jesus Christ — *the Great Refiner* — inserted His hand into Paul's life and began extracting defects and imperfections in his character that would have weakened his ministry in the future if they hadn't been dealt with, corrected, and removed.

> Receiving divine insight was enjoyable to Paul, but being changed so that revelation could operate in his life was *painful.*

Just think of how many potential leaders have been destroyed because they rose too high, too quickly. If time isn't taken to deal with the imperfections in a person's life, fame will magnify those flaws and bring that person down hard and fast.

We must thank God for the divine fire that comes to save us from the destruction we would experience if we were left to ourselves.

A CHARACTER TEST

Paul continues to say, "But as we were allowed of God *to be put in trust* with the gospel..." (1 Thessalonians 2:4).

The phrase "to be put in trust" was borrowed from the secular world. Paul knew exactly what he was doing when he used this phrase. It conveyed a truth that had taken place in his life and a principle that God requires of all would-be leaders.

Before a man could run for public office during Paul's day, he was *first* placed through a series of character tests to see if he was "fit" to be a candidate. These tests were designed to reveal who had enough character to fulfill the duties of public office if elected. If the prospective candidate failed this test, he couldn't even enter the elections.

To discover what kind of character a person possessed, the government would deliberately put him in compromising situations to see what he would do. If given the opportunity, would he lie? Would he steal? Would he be unfaithful to his country? Would he maintain a moral position, or could he be perverted by power?

Anyone who failed these tests wasn't allowed even to put his name on the ballot. *Character was everything.* If his character was too weak, he had no business in a publicly elected position where he could fall prey to those who would try to buy or manipulate him.

Now Paul is using this word to describe his own experience! All this is encompassed in the phrase "to be put in trust." Paul's words could be paraphrased as follows:

> **Before I entered the public ministry, God first tested me. He put me through three blazing, raging stages of fire that purified and burned many things out of my life. It was difficult to endure, but it was necessary to remove those wrong things in my character that would have weakened my ministry. After going through all that fire, my ministry still didn't start! The fire simply qualified me to be a candidate for the ministry!**

IT FINALLY HAPPENED

After years and years of waiting and allowing the fire of God to prepare and purify his heart, a prophetic word finally came forth to launch Paul's ministry: "...Separate me Barnabas and Saul for the work whereunto I have called them" (Acts 13:2).

I have jokingly said that by the time this prophetic word came, Paul had probably given up on the notion of public ministry, accepting the fact that he was called to be the most revelation-filled church member who ever lived!

The white-hot blaze of those years of waiting forced to the surface the last defects in Paul so Jesus could remove them. With those defects eliminated, Paul was finally ready for ministry. Only then did the word come forth that signaled it was time for his ministry to begin. All those years when Paul was waiting on the Lord, God was really waiting on *him* — waiting for his character to grow strong enough to carry the kind of ministry he was called to fulfill.

Timing belongs to the Lord, but preparation belongs to us. The stronger the ministry, the greater the fire required to prepare us.

In the future, Paul would have to endure all kinds of tests and trials involving his own people, friends, betrayers, churches that never gave him offerings, persecutions, beatings, and imprisonments. Paul would have *many* opportunities to respond to difficult situations.

> All those years when Paul was waiting on the Lord, God was really waiting on *him* — waiting for his character to grow strong enough to carry the kind of ministry he was called to fulfill.

If God hadn't dealt with Paul's attitudes *before* these trying events occurred, Paul's reactions may have been ugly and improper when confronted with them. Those defects in his personality and character may have come screaming to the top and destroyed the credibility of his ministry. That same mean, ugly Paul who existed before accepting Christ could have reemerged to defend his rights and fight for himself. His message could have been negated by his ugly, fleshly reactions.

We may not enjoy the fire of God when we feel the heat of the flames, but this kind of fire saves and delivers us. It delivers us from *us*. It saves us from the destruction that we could bring on ourselves because of wrong choices, attitudes, and impurities in our character and actions.

At least for the moment, Paul's test was over. His public ministry had finally begun. But this wasn't the end of the test. The test *never* ends. This is why Paul continues to say, "...not as pleasing men, but God, *which trieth our hearts*" (1 Thessalonians 2:4).

The word "trieth" is the same Greek word used for "allowed" at the first of the verse. Both words come from the Greek word *dokimadzo*, referring to this *intense testing by fire*.

When Paul wrote the book of First Thessalonians, it had been a long time since those years of testing in Antioch. But still he wrote in essence:*"Don't think it's over yet! God is still putting me through the fire to remove those character flaws from my life that could weaken my ministry. This process never ends!"*

TESTING COMES TO US ALL

It took years for God to make certain that Paul's inward character was strong enough for the leadership role in the Church he was called to fulfill. If this is true, shouldn't we take time as well to make sure a person is ready for the position we've asked him to fill?

Before you give a person a position of authority, *test him first.* Put him through the fire. Let that fire bring that person's imperfections to the surface and expose what is lurking down deep inside his soul.

Although this cautious approach may seem to be too lengthy and slow, it reflects your genuine concern for that person's soul. In the end, this carefulness will equip you with the knowledge of exactly who the person is and who he is not. You'll know *exactly* what you're getting. *This creates a surer foundation for the person you are considering for a position. It will also help you feel more confident about your own decision to use or not to use that person.*

In Chapter 9, I'll share my own testimony of how the fire of God first began purging my character when I was just getting started in the ministry. That holy fire initiated the process of removing those elements in my life that would have eventually weakened or destroyed my ministry. However, the process isn't over yet; the fire of God is *still* purging my character even today.

As is true with *every* person destined to be used by God in a significant way, before my ministry could become what God meant for it to be, I first had to be tested by His white-hot, burning, purging fires. *There were elements in my character that would have weakened my future ministry, so God put me in position for those character deficiencies to be removed from my life.*

QUESTIONS FOR PERSONAL GROWTH
OR GROUP DISCUSSION

1. Describe how Paul's early life as a Christian is an example of what God does to change our outward man to conform to our recreated inner man.

2. Think of your own walk with God and give an example of a time when God "put you through the fire" to remove hidden imperfections.

3. When you're facing challenging circumstances, how can you know whether you're in one of God's "seasons of testing" or enduring an attack of the enemy?

4. What is God watching for in your life as you go through a fiery test?

5. When do the seasons of testing end in your walk with God?

NOTES:

_____

_____

_____

_____

_____

_____

_____

_____

_____

_____

_____

_____

_____

_____

_____

_____

_____

_____

_____

_____

_____

_____

_____

CHAPTER 9

When God Chose Me, He Began The Process of Purifying Me With His Holy Fire!

I emphatically knew I was chosen to do something special for God when I was still a young teenager. At that time, I was full of enthusiasm and yearned for God's power to flow through me. But although I did experience manifestations of God's power, I was not at all ready for the ministry God wanted to give me. I thought I was ready, but I wasn't. Flaws needed to be removed from my character before God could begin to give me the ministry He had ordained for my life.

I distinctly remember the day in 1974 when the spirit realm opened in front of me and I saw into the future. In the flash of a second, the Spirit of God showed me the purpose of my life — "the end from the beginning," as Isaiah 46:10 says. I knew exactly where I was headed. *I knew God had chosen me!*

With that vision before me, I began to choose which school to attend, what courses to take, and what kind of education I needed to obtain in order to do what God had called me to do. I began to aggressively pursue the call of God with all my strength and might.

Once at college, I began to look for a good church where I could begin to use my spiritual gifts. As soon as I found a church, I approached the leadership and told them, "My name is Rick Renner. I'm called of God. I have a very great future ahead of me. God has revealed to me that He will use me in a great way. Should you need anyone to help you teach the Word of God, just call me, and I'll be available to you. I'm sure I would be a blessing to you."

Although that was decades ago, I still get embarrassed when I think of how aggressively I sought recognition at that young stage of my life. But God had mercifully led me to the right church. And despite my immaturity and striving for recognition, the church leadership saw the call of God on my life.

One day I received a phone call. The leaders of the church wanted to meet with me. My heart jumped! I knew this was the golden moment for which I had been waiting. They were going to hand me the pulpit and let me demonstrate my powerful anointing!

Finally, the day came for my meeting with the leadership. They opened the door, and I went in to sit down with them. I looked at them with expectation, waiting for them to thank me for my extremely anointed presence in the church. But as the conversation progressed, what I heard was *not* what I expected!

"Rick, we can see the call of God on your life. We believe that God wants to use our church to help develop that call on your life. Therefore, it's the decision of this leadership to give you a position of ministry that is very important."

When God Chose Me, He Began the Process
Of Purifying Me With His Holy Fire!

My heart was racing. The adrenaline was pumping. I was ready to pull out my calendar and mark down the date for my first public message. My great anointing was finally going to be appreciated!

"Starting next Saturday, we are placing you in charge of the cleaning crew for the church. You need to be at the church building no later than 9 a.m. because it's a big job to vacuum the carpets, dust all the furniture, set up all the chairs, and make sure all the other details are ready for Sunday's service."

I felt an ache in the pit of my stomach. It felt as if my whole world had just dropped out from under me. I was so shocked, I didn't even have words to speak. Not knowing how to respond, I thanked the church leaders for the great opportunity to serve and then left disappointed.

That meeting was on Sunday afternoon. Saturday was still six days away. During those next six days, I rehearsed the meeting I'd had with the leadership again and again in my mind. I couldn't believe they would ask someone as *spiritual* as I was to do something so menial as vacuum the carpet!

This didn't match the vision God had shown me. As a matter of fact, there wasn't anything about a carpet in that vision! So why were the church leaders asking me to do something that any regular person could do?

Finally, Saturday came.

I put on my work clothes and headed to the church building. The carpet was red and covered with stains. When I looked at the carpet and realized it was my job to clean it, I thought, *This is hopeless! This pitiful-looking carpet could never look nice, so why am I wasting my precious time and anointing on something so ludicrous?*

I shoved the chairs out of the way, plugged in the sweeper, and went to work. My attitude was rotten. I wanted to curse those stupid elders for not having more appreciation for who I was. They clearly didn't have any spiritual discernment!

But the truth is, they had *great* spiritual discernment. They *did* see the call of God on my life. They also saw a false humility, a disguised arrogance, a pride that needed to be broken and changed by God. *The fire of God was beginning to work in my life to expose serious defects in my character so I could be freed of them.*

> The fire of God was beginning to work in my life to expose serious defects in my character so I could be freed of them.

As I pushed that vacuum cleaner back and forth on that stupid red carpet, my attitude stank. It stank so bad, even I could smell it! *The fire of God was doing its job.* It was pushing my ugliness, my pride, and my rebellion to authority to the surface. I had never known what was inside me. It was a *terrible* revelation.

For the next year, I swept the carpet, washed the church dishes, cleaned the nursery, and even mowed the church lawn. I arranged the chairs in the auditorium one way, then another way, and then another way — until I finally became an expert on how to set up chairs to maximize space for more people.

God was dealing with my heart. I knew I was acting ugly. I could see how immature I had been to approach those leaders in such an arrogant way. Even if I *was* called of God and destined for a great future, I'd been stupid to promote myself in such a blatant way. *They didn't even know me!*

During that year, I learned to fast and pray. I bought a diary and began to write down the things God was doing in my heart. From the depths of my being, I yearned to better know the voice of God. So I started in earnest the process of learning how to know His voice, how to prophesy, and how to move in the gifts of the Spirit.

I cried out for God to change me. I begged for that holy fire to fall on my life and burn the chaff out of my soul. My ugly reactions to the leadership of the church had shown me another side of myself — a dreadful side that was so ugly, I was embarrassed to admit it was me!

> I cried out for God to change me. I begged for that holy fire to fall on my life and burn the chaff out of my soul.

As I pressed deeper into the things of God, my attitude began to get better. I began to sing and praise God for my job in the church! I even began to enjoy pushing that vacuum cleaner across every square inch of that auditorium. *My attitude was changing.* My soul was getting cleaned up. My character was being purified by fire. I chose to let that fire burn up the attitudes in me that I'd come to see were so wrong. I was beginning to be set free, and it felt so good!

Then the church leadership called me in for another meeting.

WHEN MY ATTITUDE GOT IN LINE, MY TEACHING MINISTRY GOT STARTED

"Rick, we can see such a change in your character. God has done an awesome work in you this past year. He has spoken to us and told us it's time to let you stand before our congregation and minister the Word of God."

Could I really be hearing this? Were my ears deceiving me? Was I really being invited to teach and preach?

By this time, I no longer saw the church leaders' invitation to teach as my special blessing *to them,* but rather as a privilege *to me.* What an honor that they would ask me to teach God's Word! Of course, I said, *"Yes!"* and began to prepare my notes.

When the date finally arrived for me to teach, I stood up in front of that congregation and taught for an hour and a half! Once I had the pulpit, I didn't want to let it go! The anointing of God really did work through me. I could sense it. The people could see it. These were my young beginnings in the ministry.

But this was not the end of God's fire; in fact, it was just the beginning. One layer of flesh had been removed, but the next layer was not going to come off as easily as the last. It would require a much *hotter* fire.

THE FIRE GETS TURNED UP A NOTCH

After college, God opened the door for me to join the staff of a huge Southern Baptist church in Arkansas. I was reared in a Baptist family, so I knew the language and behavior needed for this kind of church. Even though I spoke in tongues, I knew God was calling me to this particular church.

> One layer of flesh had been removed, but the next layer was not going to come off as easily as the last. It would require a much *hotter* fire.

What attracted me to this church was the pastor. He was incredible! I'd never heard anyone teach the Word of God as this pastor did. I sat on the front row of the church and almost drooled as I listened to him open up the Word of God to his congregation. I would literally catch myself with my mouth dropped wide open! I sat there almost hypnotized, staring in disbelief that anyone could teach the Word of God so powerfully. I had heard a lot of good Bible teachers, but never anything like this.

I was especially attracted to this pastor because he knew the Greek New Testament. In fact, I thought I'd finally found someone who knew it as well as I did! I figured that two great minds belonged together — his and mine. God made a way for me to join his staff. Soon I found myself *under* the authority of this man I respected so much.

I was gifted and smart, and I *knew* it. I was also still young and very stupid. I was so dumb that I thought the fire of God had exposed everything foul in my character while serving in the last church and that I was now as *pure* as the snow!

I'm ashamed to say it, but I was extremely impressed with myself. I was overwhelmed with my own spirituality and humility. Like the leadership of the previous church, this pastor could see the gift in my life. He could also see my pride (which I thought had been completely purged!) and my laziness.

You see, I was so gifted in certain areas, especially in matters of study and the intellect, that I didn't have to do much to be *better* than others. This is often a problem with gifted people. It doesn't take too much effort for them to be better than others, so they don't put out too much effort. Why should they? All they have to do is put forth just a little effort, and they're already ahead of the rest of the gang!

So I'd flip out my Greek New Testament, study for just a few minutes, and boom! I'd have a sermon outline that would have gotten me an "A" in any college classroom. People loved my messages. In the same way I sat dumbfounded listening to the pastor's preaching, my own young colleagues were dumbfounded by *my* messages. I was good, and I *knew* it.

So God in His wonderful wisdom placed me under this great man of God. This pastor saw what I was too blind to recognize: my arrogance, my pride, my selfishness, and my laziness. Before those character defects could be eradicated from my life, I first had to see them. *I couldn't remove what I couldn't see,* so God used this precious pastor to point my faults out to me, one by one.

God was turning up the heat a notch — and He was using this man to do it! God was putting me back into the fire to bring more impurities to the surface until they were visible even to me. Then it was up to me to *choose* to let Jesus cleanse them out of my life.

> Before those character defects could be eradicated from my life, I first had to see them. I couldn't remove what I couldn't see.

Because I'd never had to study much to do well in school, I had never developed good habits of discipline for my life. When I was in college, I might go to class, or I might not. Class attendance never seemed to determine the outcome of my grades because I did well in the subjects I enjoyed whether I went to class or not. So more often than not I'd skip class, sleeping late or fellowshipping with people from church instead of being where I was supposed to be.

My pastor saw that I hadn't developed good habits of discipline. Knowing that I'd never realize my potential if I didn't learn discipline, my pastor decided to *put* discipline into my life. He required that I meet him seven days a week at 5:30 a.m. If I was one minute late, he would scold me for being lazy and unfaithful. I was newly married and didn't *want* to be with my pastor at 5:30 a.m. I wanted to be home with Denise!

I remember throwing on my clothes as fast as I could, running down the stairs and jumping in the car at 5:20 a.m. I'd race through the streets of our city to get to that meeting. I couldn't bear to walk in and see my pastor staring at his watch — *and me* — as I walked to the table where he was waiting. I lived in mortal fear of being one minute late!

From 5:30 to 7 a.m., the pastor would lecture me on serious matters such as paying bills on time, being faithful to do what you said you'd do, being where you're supposed to be and being there on time — *never* late. Day in and day out, the pastor lectured me, trying to alert me to the fact that life is serious, not just one big game.

My pastor also required me to do things I didn't like to do, such as *visitation.* I hated that pastoral duty from the depths of my being. Nothing bored me more than driving from one end of town to the other, only to find no one at home. And when the people were home, I had to act like I was interested. I despised visitation.

My pastor gave me a weekly visitation quota that I considered totally unrealistic for anyone to meet. Each week I had to make 30 in-home visits. This quota wasn't required of anyone else on staff but me. The pastor was pressing, pushing, driving me to achieve more than I thought was even possible.

Also, every week the pastor required me to make phone calls to my Sunday school class. My division was huge, which meant I had to make a lot of phone calls. Some weeks I called more than 200 people in addition to making those required 30 in-home visits!

In addition, I was the director of the single adult ministry for the church. At that time, it was the one of the fastest growing single adult ministries in the United States. Because no other church was reaching the divorced community, I had also come up with the idea of developing a divorce recovery program. Although I've happily never been through a divorce, I knew in my heart that this was a group of people who needed to be reached. The results of that special outreach were just phenomenal. That outreach alone required most of my strength and energy.

Every Sunday morning, I was expected to wait at the altar for people from my Sunday school division who were coming to receive Christ. When the invitation began, the sweat would start rolling down my brow. The pastor would ask, *"Where are the people who received Christ this week and are supposed to make their public confession of faith today?"*

My eyes would scan the entire auditorium. If the people in my division didn't come as they had promised, my heart started sinking. Forget the fact that they needed to obey Christ and make their confession of faith public. I was thinking about Monday morning staff meeting! It was just a few short hours away. If this invitation came and went and no one from my division got saved, I was going to *suffer* for it on Monday morning. The pastor was going to hold me accountable.

The pastor required me to serve him, to carry his study books, to meet with him morning, noon, and night, and to bring needed items from the church to his home. I was also expected to drive him to meetings in Arkansas and eastern Oklahoma.

Finally, my pastor would give me preaching assignments rather than let me preach what I wanted. For instance, he required me to teach on the book of Romans. It made me so angry that someone would *tell* me what to preach! Didn't I know the voice of God as well as he? Probably not, but I *thought* I did. I knew that teaching the book of Romans would be an extremely difficult task. With everything else required of me, I didn't think I had the time needed to prepare the way I should.

I worked so hard in that church that I ended up in the hospital with a bleeding ulcer. Bags of blood had to be pumped into me intravenously. I remember my doctor telling me, "Now, Rick, we appreciate the fact that you're working so hard. But we'd like to keep you around here on earth just a little longer. You can't keep working like this. You've got to slow down."

Oh, how I wished the pastor had been in the hospital room to hear my physician's counsel! But as I lay in that bed and watched the blood run down those tubes into my arm, God began to deal with my heart. I knew deep inside that my ulcer wasn't the result of my working too hard. I was a very young man and physically capable of doing a lot of hard work.

My problem was with *my heart.*

I was complying to the pastor's wishes outwardly, but inwardly I was arguing with him all the time. I wanted every-thing done *my* way, in *my* time. Therefore, I was upset with the pastor all the time.

But the truth was, he was the pastor, and I was his associate. He had every right to ask me to do what he wanted. If he had told me to go sit on the roof of the church for a week, I should have done it with joy! I had no right to think more highly of myself than of the pastor. God had put him over me, and I was to be submitted to his authority not only in my actions, but in *my heart* as well.

I had allowed this raging war to go on inside me for a long time, and *that* is what landed me in the hospital with bags of blood being pumped into my body because of frayed nerves! My work wasn't the problem; *I* was the problem.

My pastor really wasn't doing anything wrong. He was doing what was right to teach me, discipline me, correct me, hold me accountable, push and drive me to go deeper and higher. *God loved me so much that He arranged this whole situation to change me.* But my flesh resented it, fought against it, and resisted it.

The emotions and thoughts that rose up out of my soul were so horrible, I didn't even want to look on them. They were *ugly*. I should have been grateful to this pastor, but I was very *un*grateful.

This experience revealed that there was still room for work in ol' Rick Renner. God wasn't revealing these horrible defects just so I could see them and feel sorry about them. They were being exposed so they could be *removed*. God was being good *to* me and hard *on* me at the same time.

> God wasn't revealing these horrible defects just so I could see them and feel sorry about them. They were being exposed so they could be *removed*.

That fiery season of my life was one the most merciful experiences I've ever had. The time I served under that Baptist pastor revealed the character defects that could have later weakened or even destroyed my ministry.

Like a surgeon uses his scalpel to remove the diseased area in a patient's body and thus save the patient's life, God used this pastor to reach into my character and extract diseased parts of my character I didn't even know were sick — defects that, if left unchecked, would have shortened the life of my ministry.

The fires I went through at college had removed only *a layer* of my problems. Much more was left to be removed later on, and there is still more to be removed today. The process goes on and on and on.

I could have dragged that first experience on forever and made it even more painful than it was, but I wanted to get on with my life and ministry. So I cried out to God, *"Lord, please change me! Let Your Word and fire burn up the chaff that is in my life so You can use me!"*

You see, how long we stay in the fire depends on *us*!

DOES THIS EXPERIENCE EVER END?

I have been tried by the fire of God for years now, and the fire still burns. Once in a while when God tells me to do something difficult, I still see a streak of rebellion inside me that has never been fully removed. When I recognize it, I purpose to allow the flame of God to purge it. But then just about the time I think I'm clean, another stinking attitude starts screaming up out of my soul!

> How long we stay in the fire depends on *us*!

Let me tell you, dear reader, as long as you live in this world, you will need the fire of God. This is not a devil-sent, destructive fire. This is a Holy Ghost fire that comes to purify and make you ready to be used by God.

God sends this fire because He wants you and me to be the best we can be. This is a manifestation of God's *mercy*! If we throw open our arms and receive His fire, it will change us. But if we resist the holy fire that comes to purify — if we allow those glaring defects to go unchanged — it means we have chosen to remain unusable to God. It all depends on us.

The apostle Paul was tested and changed by the fire of God. This was his testimony. I've been tested and changed by the fire of God. This is my testimony as well.

As a leader who has been tried, I'm not ashamed to say that people *need* to be tested. It is right. It is wisdom. People need to be *proven* before being used in public service or placed in leadership positions. This testing is not meant to humiliate or to hurt them. It is meant to *purify* them and to *protect* the Church.

> If we resist the holy fire that comes to purify — if we allow those glaring defects to go unchanged — it means we have chosen to remain unusable to God.

So I admonish you to examine your own heart. Ask the Holy Spirit to remove those defects that would disqualify you from the race He wants you to run. Make sure *you* are someone who is qualified to be chosen by God because your heart is right before Him.

Then once you know what God has called you to do, *never stop* until you have achieved your dream!

QUESTIONS FOR PERSONAL GROWTH OR GROUP DISCUSSION

1. Describe a time in your life when God revealed and dealt with a wrong attitude that was hurting your progress in Him.

2. What are some of the negative characteristics that the Lord has had to purge from your life over the years? Think of specific examples of how you have changed in those areas.

3. Think of an example in your own life that reveals the truth of the following statement: "How long we stay in the fire depends on *us!*"

4. Why should we look at God's process of revealing defects in our character as a *mercy* and a demonstration of His love for us?

5. When you look back on your walk with God, do you see progress and growth in the way you respond to His times of testing in your life? If not, what needs to change in your life so you can start *passing* those divine tests instead of having to *retake* them?

When God Chose Me, He Began the Process
Of Purifying Me With His Holy Fire!

NOTES:

_____

_____

_____

_____

_____

_____

_____

_____

_____

_____

_____

_____

_____

_____

_____

_____

_____

_____

_____

_____

CHAPTER 10

What To Do if
God Chooses You,
But You Feel
Like Giving Up

Forgive me for sounding so blunt, but people who quit are the biggest losers in life. They lose in every way! They held out, held on, and stayed faithful so long — but when they became physically and mentally tired, they started listening to the lies of the devil. As a result, discouragement set in, they lost the right perspective, and simply threw in the towel. How tragic to see them surrender to defeat when they are so close to winning the battle!

I can't number the people I've known through the years who were on the edge of receiving healing, only to abandon their faith at the last moment because they got discouraged. As a result of giving up and giving in to their affliction, these people are now bound by sickness. They are incarcerated in a prison of physical infirmities. All those years of waiting for their healing went right down the drain because of a moment of weakness. This is especially horrific when I realize how close they were to walking free of that devilish attack in their bodies.

I've known others who failed to answer God's call to the ministry. For years they faithfully slugged it out one step at a time, preparing for that call. They held true to what God told them to do. They resisted temptations. They rejected discouragement. They stayed right on track. Like a mother pregnant with child, they nourished that dream and waited for its birth. But when these same people were finally about to make the big breakthrough for which they had prayed and believed, they aborted that dream by giving up and terminating their stance of faith. Unfortunately, that dream was just short of its manifestation.

One of the saddest things for me is to see believers throw in the towel and quit when their faith is just about to come to maturity. You see, I understand that getting tired is a challenge. The assignments God has given me have required a lot of stamina and fortitude.

> One of the saddest things for me is to see believers throw in the towel and quit when their faith is just about to come to maturity.

The apostle Paul wrote, "Yea, so have I strived to preach the gospel, not where Christ was named, lest I should build upon another man's foundation" (Romans 15:20). Like Paul, I've been called to labor in fields where no one has worked before me. This groundbreaking, pioneering, apostolic work requires relying on God's grace and strength to put up with a lot of trouble that doesn't exist in a nation where the Gospel is already established.

I must honestly say that I've experienced moments when I felt very weak. After battling principalities, powers, governments, and religious people who also oppose the advancement of the Gospel,

I've occasionally felt like giving up and running back to America where this kind of constant onslaught doesn't exist on a daily basis.

Of course, everyone's work in every nation has its challenges, but front-line, pioneering work has challenges that are uncommon. These challenges are so peculiar that they often sound far-fetched to Westerners who possess guaranteed freedoms of religion and have never faced eviction or prosecution simply because of their faith.

In "make or break" moments when I feel drained or weak, I've learned the importance of turning to others in the Body of Christ for strength and encouragement. If we don't know how to turn to others and ask for help, it's crucial that we learn how to do it. Camaraderie with other believers is a major weapon we can draw upon to keep us in the midst of the fray until victory is certain.

James 5:16 commands us, "Confess your faults one to another, and pray one for another, that ye may be healed...." This doesn't mean we must go around groveling and groaning every time we have a bad day. Hard times come to everyone on occasion. First John 5:4 says you and I have a "faith that overcometh the world." We need to learn how to walk in this phenomenal faith that literally overrides the world system.

But if we experience a time so heavy that we feel overcome with our weaknesses, we should obey James 5:16 and go confess our need of assistance to someone else. Remember, the Bible says that if one can put a thousand to flight, two can put ten thousand to flight (Deuteronomy 32:30).

Galatians 6:2 urges us, "Bear ye one another's burdens, and so fulfil the law of Christ." The word "burden" used here describes *a burden too heavy for one person to bear alone.* You see, there are some responsibilities that only you can carry for yourself. But when you have a burden too heavy to bear alone, it's right for others to help you carry that load until you're free of it. It's better to humble yourself and admit you need help than to become so weak that you end up throwing your faith away and quitting.

> It's better to humble yourself and admit you need help than to become so weak that you end up throwing your faith away and quitting.

So don't forfeit the reward you've been confessing, dreaming, and believing to come to pass just because you're too proud to tell someone you need help. That unholy pride will take you down!

QUITTING – THE NUMBER-ONE KILLER OF DREAMS, CALLS, AND VISIONS

Quitting is the number-one killer of dreams, calls, and visions. This is why Hebrews 10:35 warns us against quitting: "Cast not away therefore your confidence, which hath great recompence of reward."

The words "cast not away" are from the Greek word *apoballo*, which is a compound of the words *apo* and *ballo*. The word *apo* means *away.* The word *ballo* means *to throw something*, such as a ball, rock, or some other item. When these two words are compounded together, it means *to throw away, discard, or get rid of something no longer desired, needed, or wanted.*

A vivid example of the word *apoballo* is used in Mark 10:50. Jesus had just finished His ministry in the city of Jericho, and He and His disciples were about to leave the city, along with the great number of people who were following Him. As Jesus passed down the road, he walked right past a blind man named Bartimaeus.

Mark 10:47,48 says, "And when he [Bartimaeus] heard that it was Jesus of Nazareth, he began to cry out, and say, Jesus, thou son of David, have mercy on me. And many charged him that he should hold his peace: but he cried the more a great deal, Thou son of David, have mercy on me." Jesus was so taken by Bartimaeus' insistence that Mark 10:49 tells us, "And Jesus stood still, and commanded him to be called...."

The word *apoballo* is found in the next verse. It says, "And he, casting away his garment, rose, and came to Jesus" (v. 50). The words "casting away" are from the word *apoballo.*

This garment was so tightly wrapped about Bartimaeus' body that it restricted him from getting to Jesus. To free himself, he took hold of that garment and *threw it out of the way.* He *discarded* it. It was a nuisance, *so he pitched it out of his way.* That garment constricted his movement and stopped him from going where he wanted to go, *so he grabbed hold of it and cast it away.*

Blind Bartimaeus was annoyed, aggravated, and exasperated by that garment that day. He wanted to get up and get to Jesus, *so he removed his garment and got it off his legs.* This removal process is the Greek word *apoballo.*

Why is this example of blind Bartimaeus so important? Because the Book of Hebrews was written to Jewish believers who had suffered much for their faith. They endured hardships but still remained faithful to the call of God and to their firm belief in His promises.

But by the time the Book of Hebrews was written, they'd been believing God to turn their tragedies into victories for multiple years. They had begun to wonder, *Is God ever going to turn our mourning into rejoicing? Is He really going to turn our ashes into beauty? How long is it going to take? Perhaps we mis-understood the promises of God. Maybe we're waiting for something that's never going to happen!*

This is why Hebrews 10:35 warns, "*Cast not away* therefore your confidence...."

The word *apoballo* suggests the Hebrew Christians were tempted to chuck the whole faith thing and forget the promises of God they'd been holding on to for so many years. They were beginning to feel that living in faith was what had restricted, bound, and kept them in the same place all those years.

Gee, if we hadn't stood on the Word all this time, at least we could have done something else with our lives, they began to reason. *Let's just forget the word God gave us. We've held on long enough. Let's toss aside what God said so we can begin to do some-thing different with our lives. It was probably just a fairy tale or a daydream anyway.*

Hebrews 10:35 is God's response to those lying accusations and doubts. God's Word admonishes, *"Don't discard, dispel, dismiss, dump, or cast off your confidence because it has great recompense of reward."*

BOLD, FRANK, OUTSPOKEN CONFESSIONS OF FAITH

The word "confidence" is the Greek word *paressia.* It refers to *boldness* and depicts *a very bold, frank, outspoken kind of language.* It was most often used in association with a tone of conversation that is *forthright, blunt, direct, and straight to the point* — a tone found only in the bravest, most fearless souls. What this type of person thinks or believes is unequivocally what he verbalizes when he speaks.

The word *paressia* was also used in connection with *political speeches.* As is true today, politicians back then made extraordinary promises of what they would accomplish if elected. Their political campaigns were built upon their *confessions* of what they would do after they assumed their newly elected post. The word *paressia* was used in a political sense to denote the *confessions* and *promises* made by candidates who verbalized their political plans and aspirations before potential voters.

It is interesting to note that the apostle Paul uses this word in First Thessalonians 2:2 when he writes about the Gospel message he proclaimed in Thessalonica. Paul writes, "...we were bold in our God to speak unto you the gospel...." The word "bold" is the word *paressia,* the same word translated "confidence" in Hebrews 10:35. Because the word *paressia* refers to a forthright, brave, fearless confession and was also used in connection with politicians' promises, this gives us insight into what and how Paul preached.

Like a politician who makes promises, the apostle Paul stood on the truth of God's Word and made loud, bold, blunt proclamations about what the Gospel would produce if his listeners would receive it, believe it, and allow it to work in their hearts and minds. Paul proclaimed promises such as *salvation* to the lost and *deliverance* to the possessed. He pledged *healing* to the sick. He promised *soundness of mind* to the mentally confused and oppressed. The apostle Paul was a "Full Gospel preacher" in the truest sense of the term. *What he believed was unequivocally what he proclaimed.*

In Romans 1:16, Paul wrote, "For I am not ashamed of the gospel of Christ: for it is the power of God unto salvation to every one that believeth...." Later, he reminded the Roman church of his style and method of preaching: "Through mighty signs and wonders, by the power of the Spirit of God; so that from Jerusalem, and round about unto Illyricum, I have fully preached the gospel of Christ" (Romans 15:19). Backed by the authority of Heaven, Paul made proclamations about God's Kingdom and His miracle-working, life-transforming power. The results of this bold, promise-making kind of preaching were *fantastic.*

Now this word *paressia* is used in Hebrews 10:35: "Cast not away therefore your confidence...." The word "confidence" evidently alludes to the bold, brave, fearless *promises, declarations,* or *confessions* these believers had made in connection with the Gospel and God's call on their lives.

Just as the apostle Paul boldly proclaimed the Gospel and its promises to an unbelieving world, these saints had been professing, declaring, and laying claim to the promises of God's Word for their personal lives. They had done it boldly. They had done it audibly. What they believed in their hearts is what they had spoken loudly and clearly to anyone who wanted to listen. However, when the results weren't forthcoming as quickly as they wanted, they were tempted to toss their faith away and count it as nonsense. But the writer of Hebrews urged them not to do it because faith "...hath great recompence of reward."

The phrase "recompense of reward" is from the Greek word *misthapodosia*. This word is a compound of two Greek words, *mistha* and *podos*. The word *mistha* is the word for *money, a person's salary*, or for *a payment that is due*. The word *podos* is the word for *foot* or *feet*. It is the root word for a *podiatrist*, which is a *foot doctor*.

When these two words are compounded, it presents a picture of money traveling by feet and headed in your direction. This is payment, recompense, a reward headed your way. One man has coined the phrase, *"Money cometh."* There is actually no better translation than this for the Greek word *misthapodosia*.

This word carries the thought of being *paid* for present labor, *reimbursed* for past expenses, provided *reparations* for past injustices, and *rewarded* at some point in the future. Let's look at each of these aspects of the word "recompense" and see how they apply to you, your dreams, and to the call of God on your life.

GOD WILL MAKE SURE
YOU ARE PAID FOR YOUR WORK OF FAITH

First of all, the phrase "recompense of reward" carries the idea of *being paid*. When a person is paid, he picks up a paycheck for work done. That paycheck reflects the effort he has put into his job. He has earned that money. It is right for him to *expect* to be paid for doing a good job. This is one meaning of the word "recompense," from the Greek word *misthapodosia*, used in Hebrews 10:35.

This verse is extremely important, because many people wrongly believe it's improper to expect a harvest from their labors. But according to this word *misthapodosia*, or "recompense of reward," God wants to fully pay His people for the hard work of faith they put forth.

God is *fair*. He is *equitable* in His dealings. If you have given your best and worked with all your heart and might to fulfill His call, He will make certain you are paid for what you've done. God never overlooks what you do for Him. Hebrews 6:10 says, "For God is not unrighteous to forget your work and labour of love, which ye have shewed toward his name...."

The apostle Paul said it this way: "The husbandman that laboureth must be first partaker of the fruits" (2 Timothy 2:6). This is the picture of a farmer who labors in his vineyard. The word "labor" is the word *kopos*. It always refers to *the hardest, most physical kind of labor*.

In fact, this particular verse pictures a man working out in his vineyard, breaking up the hardened soil and trimming the vines. Perspiration runs down his brow as a result of the harsh sunlight and severe climate.

> **God never overlooks what you do for Him.**

This man is committed to his labor. He works and tends to his vines regardless of the weather conditions. He knows that the success of his vineyards depends on the level of his involvement and devotion.

Likewise, when you put your whole heart into the project God gave to you, making no fuss about the heat or the severe climate you find yourself in at the moment, it is right and just for you to be "first partaker of the fruits" as well.

When it's time to pick the fruit, harvest the fields, and eat the fruit of the vine or crops, God promises that the hardest workers will be the first to pull up to the table and enjoy the meal. *Their level of commitment guarantees their right to the first pick of everything, leaving the leftovers for those who were less serious about the task.*

God pays you by giving you victories in different areas of your life. That pay may be success in your ministry. It may be financial. It may be a greater anointing than you've ever had. It may be a phenomenal increase of prosperity. It may be that God pays you by providing a long-term friendship you'll be able to count on for years to come.

God has all kinds of ways to recompense us for staying in faith and doing what He called us to do. But one thing is for sure —

> God has all kinds of ways to recompense us for staying in faith and doing what He called us to do.

the word *misthapodosia* proves that God wants you and me to receive a blessing for the services we have rendered in His Kingdom.

Thank God for Heaven! You'll receive a future reward there too. But right now you're here on planet earth, with physical and material needs that must be met. You need blessings and help right now to live and take care of your personal responsibilities. The devil may try to hinder God's blessings from arriving at your doorstep, but don't give up! It's right for you to expect to receive payment for your labors even now.

God has riches in glory especially reserved to meet your current needs (Philippians 4:19). And there's no need to be beggarly in how much you expect to be blessed either. These riches in glory are reserved for *you*, so raise your level of expectation! Throw open your arms! It's time for you to receive the harvest you *earned* through a lot of hard work and sowing!

The apostle Paul asked the rhetorical questions, "Who goeth a warfare any time at his own charges? who planteth a vineyard, and eateth not of the fruit thereof? or who feedeth a flock, and eateth not of the milk of the flock?" (1 Corinthians 9:7).

This was Paul's answer to those who said it wasn't right to expect a harvest from our spiritual labors. Paul corrected that nonsensical thinking real fast. He said it's normal to expect God to reward us for work done. This is something God *wants* to do for us!

If something has been telling your mind it's not right to expect God to reward you for your faith in this life, tell that religious spirit to get off you! Open your heart *right now* and expect God to recompense you for services rendered in your walk of faith. Remember, *faith produces results in every realm of life.*

GOD WANTS TO REIMBURSE YOU
FOR PAST INCONVENIENCES AND EXPENSES

The phrase "recompense of reward" also carries the idea of *being reimbursed for an expense that a person has paid out of his own pocket in order to get his job done.* Perhaps the company had no available cash, so this employee put his own money on the table. He willingly gave of his own resources, at least temporarily, to cover the costs and needs of the organization.

It would have been better if he'd had an expense account to handle these needs. But because the money wasn't available at the time, he covered the cost himself. Now it's time to tally up the total amount owed to him so he can be *recompensed* for what he willingly contributed at a difficult or inconvenient moment.

The Lord sees and remembers when you take a costly stand of faith. Psalm 56:8 says He knows every tear you shed. He even keeps those tears in a bottle! The same verse says He has kept a record of all the difficulties you've encountered along the way.

Then in Psalm 139:3, it says God knows when you get up, and He knows when you lie down. He's acquainted with all your ways. Before you speak a word, He knows what you're going to say. He even knows your thoughts. In fact, there's nothing He doesn't see or know about you. Hebrews 4:13 declares that "…all things are naked and opened unto the eyes of him with whom we have to do."

> **The Lord sees and remembers when you take a costly stand of faith.**

If you ever invested time, money, energy, and commitment into God's Kingdom that no one knew about except you and the Lord, it did *not* go unnoticed. The Lord saw it all.

You may be tempted to feel like you've wasted years waiting for your calling or dream to come to pass. But don't allow fleshly thoughts to suck you down into a mire of self-pity and defeat. God will reward you for all you've sacrificed and forfeited along the way. He will make sure you're reimbursed for all the love and patience you've shown and all the time, energy, commitment, and money you've given over the years.

GOD WANTS TO MAKE REPARATIONS FOR THE WARS YOU'VE BEEN THROUGH

The phrase "recompense of reward" also means *to make reparation*. The word "reparation" means *to make amends for wrong or injury done in the past*.

Nations make *war reparations* to compensate or make amends for the destruction and damage they wreaked upon each other. An example is the reparation payments modern-day Germany is still making to Israel for the mass murder of Jews during the Holocaust. Germany has paid multiple millions of dollars to the State of Israel to make amends for its actions during World War II.

This tells us that God intends to make up for all the devil has tried to do to you along the way of faith and obedience. You may have thought you lost it all, but in reality you have lost nothing because God will make sure reparations are made to recompense you for all that's been lost through the years. If you will hold on to your call or dream and refuse to cast it away, He'll make reparations for you and ensure that everything works out all right!

> God intends to make up for all the devil has tried to do to you along the way of faith and obedience.

Often when people wait for their calling or dream to come to pass, they sacrifice things that others are not called on to sacrifice. They frequently forfeit the comforts of life. They let golden opportunities pass them by in order to stay focused on what they believe is right for them. They relinquish possessions; they give up their reputations — all because they are standing in faith for the fulfillment of their God-given dream.

Many great Old Testament men and women did this, such as Noah, Job, Abraham, Moses, and so on. At the moment of sacrifice, their flesh may have felt deprived and wounded. But in the end, God moved so dramatically in their lives that they each ended up becoming a glorious winner in the arena of faith.

Everything Job ever sacrificed was repaid to him, and even more. Everything Moses forfeited when he left Egypt, God repaid to him, giving Moses even greater power and authority than he could have ever had if he'd stayed in Egypt. All that Noah relinquished to fulfill his call — his reputation in the eyes of a scoffing world, the time and energy he devoted to building the ark, the investments he made into his calling — all this and even more was repaid to him when the waters of the flood decreased and he became the sole inheritor of planet earth.

Things may seem a little tough in your own life at the moment, but that's only a temporary condition. The apostle Paul wrote, "For our light affliction, which is but for a moment, worketh for us a far more exceeding and eternal weight of glory" (2 Corinthians 4:17).

Considering the problems Paul had been dragged through to do the will of God, it's amazing that he'd call his difficulties a mere *"light affliction."* But Paul knew that if he'd hold tight, hang on, and keep doing what God told him to do, it would eventually produce "...a far more exceeding and eternal weight of glory."

This phrase describes an overshooting, magnificent, heavy-weight presence of God's glory in Paul's life and ministry. It was on this that Paul kept his focus, not on the problems he encountered.

Likewise, we must be careful not to fixate on the hazards and formidable tasks before us. Rather, we must focus on the ultimate victory our faith will win if we hold on and endure to the end. *God will make sure we are properly taken care of as we hold fast to the confession of our faith without wavering* (Hebrews 10:23).

GOD WANTS TO REWARD YOU
IN THE FUTURE

The phrase "recompense of reward" also points to *a future prize.* The Bible is loaded with verses and promises about future rewards that will be distributed to the saints. One thing is clear: Those who have labored fervently and sincerely for the Lord will be richly rewarded for their endeavors in Heaven.

In Second Timothy 4:6-8, the apostle Paul spoke of the reward that was laid up in Heaven for him. Paul anticipated the day when he would see the Lord and receive the reward for his life's labors: "For I am now ready to be offered, and the time of my departure is at hand. I have fought a good fight, I have finished my course, I have kept the faith: Henceforth there is laid up for me a crown of righteousness, which the Lord, the righteous judge, shall give me at that day: and not to me only, but unto all them also that love his appearing."

Paul lived his entire life with this prospect of a heavenly reward before him. He knew that one day he would stand before Jesus and give account for his life and ministry. This future moment was so real to him, it became part of the driving motivation that kept him going even through troubled, difficult times.

I can think of so many people who didn't follow Paul's example. They were so close to obtaining great victories in their lives, but they lost sight of the eternal rewards being laid up in Heaven for them.

I've personally learned that when I remember that future moment — the moment I will look into the eyes of Jesus to be rewarded or judged for what I did or did not do with my gifts and callings — it gives me strength to endure to the end.

> When I remember that future moment — the moment I will look into the eyes of Jesus to be rewarded or judged for what I did or did not do with my gifts and callings — it gives me strength to endure to the end.

In Revelation 22:12, Jesus says, "And, behold, I come quickly; and my reward is with me, to give every man according as his work shall be."

We must never lose sight of the fact that there is a future prize reserved for those who hold on to their calling and who do what God told them to do. Those who stay in faith are the ones who will rejoice on the day they see Jesus!

DILIGENCE IS REQUIRED
FOR YOUR CALLING TO COME TO PASS

Some people are just lazy, which is why they never see anything accomplished with their lives. They blame their lack of success on this, that, and everything but themselves.

But ultimately we are all responsible for our success or for our lack of it. We all have the same promises, the same faith, the same power, and the same Jesus who sits at the right hand of God to make intercession for us (Hebrews 7:25).

> Ultimately we are all responsible for our success or for our lack of it.

God is no respecter of persons. What He does for one, He will do for all. What makes the difference is not God, but the individual person's level of determination.

Hebrews 11:6 says that God "…is a rewarder of them that *diligently* seek him." According to this verse, "diligence" is required for your dream, vision, or calling to come to pass.

The word "diligence" in Greek carries an entire range of power-packed meanings. It means *to zealously seek for something with all of one's heart, strength, and mind.* It also reflects the ideas of being *hard-working, attentive, busy, constant, and persistent in one's devotion to what he or she is doing.* Let's look at these words to understand what diligence *is* and *is not.*

HARD-WORKING

A lazy, neglectful attitude will never get you where you need to go. If you take your life assignment lightly — if you approach it with a casual, easygoing, take-it-easy, relaxed attitude — you'll never go far in the fulfillment of your call or dream. Live like a slug, and you'll eat dirt the rest of your life.

Make the decision to get up, get off your nincompoop lazy bone, crucify your flesh, and put your hand to the plow! Jesus said, "…No man, having put his hand to the plough, and looking back, is fit for the kingdom of God" (Luke 9:62). It takes hard work to achieve anything, and complaining about it won't make it any easier.

So if you're serious about living *in faith*, it's time for you to adjust your level of commitment and get to work! Being a hard worker is a part of being diligent.

ATTENTIVE

If you want your faith to be rewarded, you must give your *full attention* to what God has called you to do. Living in faith cannot be a sideline issue. It must have your full consideration, your undivided attention, and your mental and spiritual concentration. Ceaseless, around-the-clock, nonstop devotion is essential in order for you to be diligent.

> If you want your faith to be rewarded, you must give your *full attention* to what God has called you to do.

BUSY

Living in faith will keep you occupied! You won't have time for wrong attitudes and wrong thinking. To stay in faith, you must be engrossed, totally absorbed, and fully engaged. You must immerse yourself in faith, prayer, and meditation regarding God's call on your life. *Distractions are not allowed.* It takes 100 percent of your effort for you to accomplish what God puts in your heart. This is also part of being diligent.

CONSTANT

Fickle, flighty, erratic behavior will never produce the fulfillment of God's will in your life. It takes consistency and determination to push the powers of hell aside and obtain the victory you've desired.

If you wander back and forth and in and out of faith, fluctuating this way and that, you'll never reap anything enduring for the Kingdom of God. To produce powerful results, you must be *constant* in your commitment. You must be even, "steady-as-she-goes," fixed, unchanging, and steadfast. It's all part of being diligent.

PERSISTENT

When a person is persistent, he refuses to relent. He's stubborn even in the face of opposition and unbending until his objective is achieved.

Withstanding opposition and braving adversity is just a part of the walk of faith. In order for you to resist attempts to abort your dream, you must also be *persistent*. This is the kind of commitment required to live and walk in faith.

I'll guarantee you that if you are actually living *in faith*, you *persistently* pursued it! Therefore, Hebrews 11:6 could be read, *"God is a rewarder of those who are hard-working, attentive, busy, constant, and persistent in their pursuit of seeking God."*

WHAT LIES IN YOUR FUTURE
IF YOU CHOOSE TO GIVE UP AND QUIT?

Hebrews 10:38,39 says, "Now the just shall live by faith: but if any man draw back, my soul shall have no pleasure in him. But we are not of them that draw back unto perdition...." These verses tell us *explicitly* what happens to people who walk away from what God called them to do. The ramifications are grim and ghastly.

The words "draw back" are taken from the Greek word *hupostellomai*. It means *to draw back, to withdraw from something that has already been started*, or *to shrink back*. This is the idea of a person who starts on a journey and then abruptly reverses his direction. He is now moving backwards. He is *backing out* of a previously held position or some prior commitment.

The word "perdition" is the Greek word *apoleia*. It describes *something so ruined and rotten that it is decomposing*, such as rotten potatoes that have sat too long and are now spoiled and ruined.

Frequently this word was used to describe the stench of a decaying animal or a dead human body. It's a loathsome, putrid, vulgar, disgusting scent that is *nauseating*. One whiff leaves you with a sick feeling in the pit of your stomach. The smell is so repulsive that you feel like running to the bathroom to vomit.

This portrayal pretty well gives you the picture of what happens when a person walks away from the call of God. Things in his life turn *pretty stinky*.

Once I was invited to have lunch with a minister who had been associated with many great men and women of faith. He had worked on staff for a large, successful ministry before leaving to start his own ministry.

However, when this man's ministry didn't grow as fast as he wished, he became discouraged and depressed. He began questioning everything he believed. He wasn't experiencing the victory he expected, so he began to measure what he *believed* by what he was *experiencing*.

People often throw in the towel and quit when they don't see results as quickly as they want. I am amazed at how short-lived some people's faith is. If their prayers for healing aren't quickly answered, they allow their flesh to suck them down to the low-level conclusion that it must be God's will for them to be sick. Or if they sow their finances, believing for a financial harvest, but don't see that harvest in a matter of months, they are tempted to plunge into thinking that what they were taught about prosperity must be wrong. The problem is, they want "microwave answers" to problems they took a long time to create. *They need to give their faith time to work!*

Most people quit before their faith has time to work. These folks need a good dosage of patience to go along with their faith!

FAITH AND PATIENCE ARE PARTNERS

You see, faith and patience are *partners*. You need both to receive the promises of God. You also need both to fulfill God's will for your life. Hebrews 10:36 says, "For ye have need of patience, that, after ye have done the will of God, ye might receive the promise."

> Most people quit before their faith has time to work.

The word "patience" comes from the word *hupomene*. The Early Church called *hupomene* the "queen of all virtues." They believed that if a person possessed this virtue, he would ultimately succeed at any venture he undertook.

The word *hupomene* is a compound of the words *hupo* and *meno*. The word *meno* is the primary root of the word and it means *to stay, to remain, to continue,* or *to permanently abide.* It is the very word Jesus uses in John 15:7, when He says, "If ye abide in me, and my words abide in you, ye shall ask what ye will, and it shall be done unto you."

When the apostle John wrote this verse, he used the word *meno* to describe "abiding" in the Lord. A literal translation would be *"If you steadfastly and continuously abide in Me, and if My words steadfastly and continuously abide in you, you may ask what you will, and it shall be done for you."*

But the picture changes radically when you add the prefix *hupo* at the beginning of the word. The word *hupo* means "under" and in certain cases means "alongside." Compound this with *meno*, and it is the picture of a person who is under (*hupo*) something, such as *a heavy load.* But this person has resolved that he is going to stay (*meno*) in that one spot, regardless how hard or heavy that load gets.

This person is *thoroughly committed* to maintaining his position. He will stay under that load as long it's necessary for him to achieve victory. He is intent on standing by his commitment, regardless of the cost he must pay. Nothing can sway or move him to change his mind. He is not going to relinquish his territory!

One well-known Greek scholar says *hupomene* would be better translated "endurance." That is correct! This is an attitude that *never gives up*!

I call this quality "bulldog faith." It is a faith that manifests as a tough, resistant, persistent, obstinate, stubborn, tenacious spirit that refuses to let go of what it wants or believes. I personally translate the word *hupomene* as "hang-in-there power"!

The Early Church understood the power of this type of patience. They were up against the powers of hell as they resisted the aggression of an evil Roman empire. These early Christians didn't have Bible school degrees or diplomas to lean on or wave in the faces of the authorities. They had no legal protection guaranteed by a constitution. There were no Christian lawyers or politicians to turn to for their defense.

But these believers understood that if they stood their ground long enough, the devil would eventually back off and leave them alone. No wonder they called *hupomene* the "queen of all virtues"!

You, too, must have *hupomene* ("patience") if you intend to beat the devil at his game and successfully do what God has called you to do. If *hupomene* is working in your life, then it's just a matter of time until victory comes to you. It's not a question of *if* your victory will come. It's only a question of *when*. This *hupomene* power is essential if you intend to stay in the fight until your enemies are under your feet and you reign supreme!

DON'T LET THE DEVIL TALK YOU INTO GIVING UP

So don't let loose of your faith! The day your vision dies is the day your joy will disappear and life will become pointless. You'll end up in "perdition" (*see* pages 320-321 for a refreshing on the word "perdition") if you let go of that word God gave you. You'll start putting out the putrid stench of a faith turned *sour*.

The minister I had lunch with is a perfect example of someone whose faith turned sour. Instead of resisting the lies the devil was speaking to him and maintaining his stand on the Word, this minister relinquished his position of faith and gave place to doubt and unbelief in his mind.

Before long, this man's mind was so filled with questions and doubts that he even began questioning the motives of those who preached a victorious message. He'd ask, *If the walk of faith is real, why am I not experiencing it?* His walk of faith would have worked for him if he had just held on, but because he let go, he lost his battle and became bitter.

Seated before me that day was a man who had turned around and backed out of the life of faith he had once embraced. His whole mind was doused in defeat. He had even rationalized his defeat to himself by immersing himself in a doctrinal system designed to support his depressing experience.

The entire conversation with this minister just made me feel *ill.* It was *sickening.* He even looked poor, sick, and defeated. That pathetic, depressing spirit had gotten hold of him and suppressed his whole countenance.

This is why Hebrews 10:38 says, "...if any man draw back, my soul shall have no pleasure in him." It isn't a pleasurable experience to see someone who once made such advances later take a turn for the worse. In fact, it's heartbreaking!

But let's take this to another level that you can relate to yourself. Perhaps you can think of some people you know who once intensely wanted to do the will of God. They believed in what God called them to do.

But when it didn't turn out the way these people expected and they hit a few bumps along the way, they said, *"Forget this faith thing. It doesn't work!"* They *turned around* and *backed up* from the thing God called them to do. Before this, they were experiencing an adventurous walk of faith. They had so much going for them — so much potential!

Isn't it heartbreaking to see what happens to people like this? It's especially sad when you know the potential of what they could have become if they'd just held on a little longer.

These people are on a track that is going to lead them to defeat and despair for the rest of their lives unless they repent, turn around, and get back on track again. It's "perdition" for them if they don't put on the brakes!

Is God Pointing His Finger at You Today?

Perhaps you are the one who once tried to do God's will but then allowed yourself to become discouraged and defeated. You threw in the towel. You let the devil have his way in ruining your dream. You gave up, turned back, and withdrew from doing what you were called to do. If that's you, you're probably disgusted with yourself. You're feeling unhappy and unfulfilled, right?

Well, there's no need for you to remain in this miserable condition for the rest of your life. God is pointing His finger at you today, calling you to do something:

Bigger than your natural talents.

Bigger than your natural gifts.

Bigger than your experience.

You need to stop living in fear of failure and just say, *"YES!"*

That "yes" will throw open the door to the most adventurous life you've ever known. *You'll forget the doldrums!* Your life will take on a whole new flare! It will be so full and so rich that you'll never want to turn back. And after tasting the feast God longs to set before you, you'll never hesitate to obey Him again. As a matter of fact, you'll *jump* when God calls you to take the next big step of faith!

The table is prepared, and the meal is cooked. But God is waiting for *you* to pull your chair up to the table, pick up your knife and fork, and begin digging into the awesome plan He has for your life!

> After tasting the feast God longs to set before you, you'll never hesitate to obey Him again.

In moments like this, you could give God 1,000 reasons why He shouldn't use you. As Moses did when God first called him, you could argue that you can't speak well enough, aren't talented enough, or don't have enough gifts or experience. But when you've run out of arguments and excuses to throw at God, you'll still know the truth deep down inside. God is speaking to you, beckoning you to step out into new, unknown territory. He's challenging you to do something exciting, adventurous, and momentous for Him. He is waiting for your answer — *yes or no?*

What has God told you to do? Has He spoken to your heart? Did you reason away His message to you, telling yourself that it must have just been your imagination because God surely wouldn't choose someone like you? Did you let the devil talk you out of your mission because it sounded too grand and glorious for someone like you?

Living in faith begins the day God reveals His purpose to you. But *staying in faith* demands the greatest level of commitment and determination. To quit before the job is done is the equivalent of moving *out of* faith. *Dear friend, don't let that happen to you!* Don't let discouragement keep you from holding fast to the call God gave you. Hold fast! Stay put! *Don't stop until you've done exactly what God has told you to do.*

Staying in faith as you obey God's call requires a stubborn, obstinate, determined, committed, diehard attitude. If you're just going to "give it your best shot" or "try it for a while," you'll

> Don't let discouragement keep you from holding fast to the call God gave you.

never make it. You must make the quality decision that you'll never quit or abandon your God-given dream until you've accomplished it just the way God wanted it done.

Too much depends on you for you to throw in the towel and quit now. *Anyone can quit!* God is calling you to stand your ground until the job is complete. The hardship you're experiencing is only temporary. Shift your focus off fleeting emotional feelings and momentary discomfort, and redirect your concentration to the eternal investments you're making in the realm of God's Spirit.

Aches and pains are soon forgotten when the powers of hell move out of the way and your dream becomes a manifested reality. When that happens, you'll be glad you didn't take the easy road and join the club of quitters. Instead, you said *yes* to God and made Him glad that He chose *you!*

QUESTIONS FOR PERSONAL GROWTH OR GROUP DISCUSSION

1. What is the number-one killer of dreams, calls, and visions?

2. What are some of the consequences people suffer when they give up on God's plan for their lives?

3. Why is it important to turn to others for help and encouragement in those "make or break" moments?

4. Explain the significance of Bartimaeus' example when you're feeling tempted to give up on your dream.

5. Think of a time when God recompensed you for a costly stand of faith you had taken. In what form did that "divine compensation" come?

NOTES:

_____

_____

_____

_____

_____

_____

_____

_____

_____

_____

_____

_____

_____

_____

_____

_____

_____

_____

_____

_____

_____

REFERENCE BOOK LIST

1. How To Use New Testament Greek Study Aids by Walter Jerry Clark (Loizeaux Brothers).

2. Strong's Exhaustive Concordance of the Bible by James H. Strong.

3. The Interlinear Greek-English New Testament by George Ricker Berry (Baker Book House).

4. The Englishman's Greek Concordance of the New Testament by George Wigram (Hendrickson).

5. New Thayer's Greek-English Lexicon of the New Testament by Joseph Thayer (Hendrickson).

6. The Expanded Vine's Expository Dictionary of New Testament Words by W. E. Vine (Bethany).

7. Theological Dictionary of the New Testament by Geoffrey Bromiley; Gephard Kittle, ed. (Eerdmans).

8. The New Analytical Greek Lexicon; Wesley Perschbacher, ed. (Hendrickson).

9. The New Linguistic and Exegetical Key to the Greek New Testament by Cleon Rogers Jr. (Zondervan).

10. Word Studies in the Greek New Testament by Kenneth Wuest, 4 Volumes (Eerdmans).

11. New Testament Words by William Barclay (Westminster Press).

12. Word Meanings by Ralph Earle (Hendrickson).

13. International Critical Commentary Series; J. A. Emerton, C. E. B. Cranfield, and G. N. Stanton, eds. (T. & T. Clark International).

14. Vincent's Word Studies of the New Testament by Marvin R. Vincent, 4 Volumes (Hendrickson).

15. New International Dictionary of New Testament Theology; Verlyn D. Verbrugge, ed. (Zondervan).

Prayer of Salvation

When Jesus Christ comes into your life, you are immediately emancipated — totally set free from the bondage of sin!

If you have never received Jesus as your personal Savior, it is time to experience this new life for yourself! The first step to freedom is simple. Just pray this prayer from your heart:

Lord, I can never adequately thank You for all You did for me on the Cross. I am so undeserving, Jesus, but You came and gave Your life for me anyway. I repent and turn from my sins right now, Jesus. I receive You as my Savior, and I ask You to wash away my sin by Your precious blood. I thank You from the depths of my heart for doing what no one else could do for me. Had it not been for Your willingness to lay down Your life for me, I would be eternally lost.

Thank You, Jesus, that I am now redeemed by Your blood. You bore my sin, my sickness, my pain, my lack of peace, and my suffering on the Cross. Your blood has covered my sin, washed me whiter than snow, and given me rightstanding with the Father. I have no need to be ashamed of my past sins, because I am now a new creature in You. Old things have passed away, and all things have become new because I am in Jesus Christ (1 Corinthians 5:17).

Because of You, Jesus, today I am forgiven; I am filled with peace; and I am a joint heir with You! Satan no longer has a right to lay any claim on me. From a grateful heart, I will faithfully serve You the rest of my days!

If you prayed this prayer from your heart, something amazing has happened to you. No longer a servant to sin, you are now a servant of Almighty God. The evil spirits that once exacted every ounce of your being and required your all-inclusive servitude no longer possess the authorization to control you or to dictate your destiny.

If you prayed this prayer from your heart, something amazing has happened to you. No longer a servant to sin, you are now a servant of Almighty God. The evil spirits that once exacted every ounce of your being and required your all-inclusive servitude no longer possess the authorization to control you or to dictate your destiny.

As a result of your decision to turn your life over to Jesus Christ, your eternal home has been decided forever. HEAVEN is now your permanent address.

God's Spirit has moved into your own human spirit, and you have become the "temple of God" (1 Corinthians 6:19). What a miracle! To think that God, by His Spirit, now lives inside of you! I have never ceased to be amazed at this incredible miracle of God in my own life. He gave me (and you!) a new heart and then made us His home!

Now you have a new Lord and Master, and His name is Jesus. From this moment on, the Spirit of God will work in you and supernaturally energize you to fulfill God's will for your life. Everything will change for you now — and it's all going to change for the best!

If you prayed this prayer for the first time, please call or email our Renner Ministries office.
We would love to pray with you!

Phone: 918-496-3213
Email: **prayer@renner.org**.

ABOUT THE AUTHOR

Rick Renner is a respected leader and teacher within the Christian community, both in the U.S. and abroad. He fills a unique position in the modern Christian world, combining an extraordinary depth of scriptural and practical knowledge with an easy-to-understand, faith-filled approach to the Bible. Rick became passionate about the Greek New Testament when studying Journalism and Classical Greek as a university student. In the years that followed, he continued his extensive study of the Greek New Testament, later earning a Doctor of Philosophy in Ministry.

Along with his wife Denise and their sons and families, Rick works to see the Gospel preached, leadership trained, and churches established throughout the world. Together, their global mission is to teach, strengthen, and rescue. Rick is the founder of the *Good News Television Network* (aka *Media Mir*), the first Christian television network established in the former Soviet Union that today broadcasts the Gospel to a potential audience of 110 million people. His broadcast "Good News With Rick Renner" can be seen across the entire former USSR. Rick has distributed hundreds of thousands of teaching audio and videotapes, and his best-selling books have been translated into four major languages. In addition, Rick teaches via the Internet with English-speaking broadcasts.

Rick is the founder of the *"It's Possible"* humanitarian foundation, an organization committed to providing for the practical needs of various segments of Russian society. He is also the founder of the *Good News Association of Pastors and Churches*, through which he oversees and strengthens hundreds of churches throughout the former Soviet Union. In addition, Rick and Denise pastor the thriving *Moscow Good News Church*, located in the very heart of Moscow, Russia. *RENNER Ministries* has offices in Russia, Ukraine, Latvia, England, and the United States. Rick resides in Moscow with his wife and their three sons and families.

ABOUT OUR WORK
IN THE FORMER USSR

From inception to its current role in the Body of Christ, *RENNER Ministries'* purpose and vision has been to teach, strengthen, and rescue people for the Kingdom of God. Although the Renners' ministry began much earlier, in 1991 God called Rick and Denise Renner and their family to what is now the former Soviet Union. Since that time, millions of lives have been touched by the various outreaches of *RENNER Ministries*. Nevertheless, the Renners' ever-increasing vision for this region of the world continues to expand across 11 time zones to reach 300 million precious souls for God's Kingdom.

The *Moscow Good News Church* was begun in September 2000 in the very heart of Moscow, right next to Red Square. Since that time, the church has grown to become one of the largest Protestant churches in Moscow and a strategic model for pastors throughout this region of the world to learn from and emulate. Today the outreaches of the *Moscow Good News Church* includes ministry to families, senior citizens, children, youth, and international church members, as well as a special-ized ministry to businesspeople and an outreach to the poor and needy. Rick and Denise also founded churches in Riga, Latvia, and in Kiev, Ukraine, both of which continue to thrive.

Part of the mission of *RENNER Ministries* is to come alongside pastors and ministers and take them to a higher level of excellence and professionalism in the ministry. Therefore, since 1991 when the walls of Communism first collapsed, this ministry has been working in the former USSR to train and equip pastors, church leaders, and ministers, helping them attain the necessary skills and knowledge to fulfill the ministries that the Lord has given to them.

To this end, Rick Renner founded both a seminary and a ministerial association. The *Good News Seminary* is a school that operates as a part of the *Moscow Good News Church*. It specializes in training leaders to start new churches all over the former Soviet Union. The *Good News Association of Pastors and Churches* is a church-planting and church-supporting organization with a membership of pastors and churches that numbers in the hundreds.

RENNER Ministries also owns and operates the *Good News Television Network*, the first and one of the largest TV outreaches within the territory of the former USSR. Since its inception in 1992, this television network has become one of the strongest instruments available today for declaring the Word of God to the 15 nations of the former Soviet Union, reaching 110 million potential viewers every day with the Gospel of Jesus Christ.

In addition, Rick Renner also founded the *"It's Possible!"* humanitarian foundation, which is involved in various outreaches in the city of Moscow. The *"It's Possible"* foundation uses innovative methods to help different age groups of people who are in great need.

If you would like to learn more about our work in the former Soviet Union, please visit our website at www.renner.org, or call 918-496-3213.

INSTITUTE BOOKS, INC.

Teaching you can trust.

A Division of Renner Institute, Inc.

8316 E. 73rd St., Suite 207

Tulsa, OK 74133

Phone: 918-893-3433

Fax: 918-893-2444

Email: contact@rennerinstitute.com

A LIGHT IN DARKNESS
VOLUME ONE

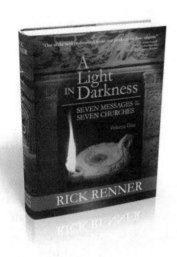

Step into the world of the First Century Church as Rick Renner creates a panoramic experience of unsurpassed detail to transport you into the ancient lands of the seven churches of Asia Minor. Within the context of this fascinating — and, at times, shocking — historical backdrop, Rick outlines challenges early believers faced in taking the Gospel to a pagan world. After presenting a riveting account of the apostle John's vision of the exalted Christ, Rick leads you through an in-depth study of Jesus' messages to the churches of Ephesus and Smyrna — profoundly relevant messages that still resonate for His Church today.

$79.95 (Hardback)
ISBN 978-0-9779459-8-6

Rick's richly detailed historical narrative, enhanced by classic artwork and superb photographs shot on location at archeological sites, will make the lands and the message of the Bible come alive to you as never before. Parallels between Roman society of the First Century and the modern world prove the current relevance of Christ's warning and instructions.

A Light in Darkness is an extraordinary book series that will endure and speak to generations to come. This authoritative first volume is a virtual encyclopedia of knowledge — a definitive *go-to* resource for any student of the Bible and a classic *must-have* for Christian families everywhere.

Faced with daunting challenges, the modern Church *must* give urgent heed to what the Holy Spirit is saying in order to be equipped for the end of this age.

For more information, visit us online at: **www.renner.org**
Book Resellers: Contact Harrison House at 800-888-4126,
or visit **www.harrisonhouse.com** for quantity discounts.

MINING THE TREASURES
OF GOD'S WORD

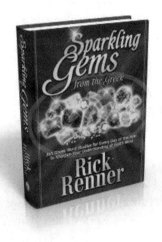

Author Rick Renner unearths a rich treasure trove of truths in his remarkable devotional, *Sparkling Gems From the Greek.* Drawing from an extensive study of both the Bible and New Testament Greek, Rick illuminates 365 passages with more than 1,285 in-depth Greek word studies. Far from intellectualizing, he blends his solid instruction with practical applications and refreshing insights. Find challenge, reassurance, comfort, and reminders of God's abiding love and healing every day of the year.

$34.95 (Hardback)
ISBN: 978-0-9725454-2-6

Sparkling Gems From the Greek Electronic Reference Edition

Now you are only a few short clicks away from discovering the untold riches of God's Word! Offering embedded links to three exhaustive indices for ultimate ease in cross-referencing scriptures and Greek word studies, this unique computer study tool gives you both convenience and portability as you read and explore Rick Renner's one-of-a-kind daily devotional!

$29.95 (CD-ROM)
ISBN: 978-0-9725454-7-1

A BIBLICAL APPROACH
TO SPIRITUAL WARFARE

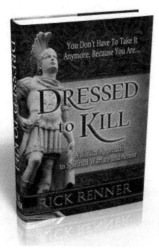

Rick Renner's book *Dressed To Kill* is considered by many to be a true classic on the subject of scriptural warfare. The original version, which sold more than 400,000 copies, is a curriculum staple in Bible schools worldwide. In this beautifully bound hardback volume, you will find:

- 512 pages of reedited text

- 16 pages of full-color illustrations

- Questions at the end of each chapter to guide you into deeper study

$24.95 (Hardback)
ISBN: 978-0-9779459-0-0

In *Dressed To Kill*, Rick explains with exacting detail the purpose and function of each piece of Roman armor. In the process, he describes the significance of our *spiritual* armor not only to withstand the onslaughts of the enemy and but also to overturn the tendencies of the carnal mind. Furthermore, Rick delivers a clear, scriptural presentation on the biblical definition of spiritual warfare — what it is and what it is not.

When you walk with God in deliberate, continual fellowship, He will enrobe you with Himself. Armed with the knowledge of who you are in Him, you will be dressed and dangerous to the works of darkness, unflinching in the face of conflict, and fully equipped to take the offensive and gain mastery over any opposition from your spiritual foe. You don't have to accept defeat anymore once you are *dressed to kill!*

For more information, visit us online at: **www.renner.org**
Book Resellers: Contact Harrison House at 800-888-4126,
or visit **www.harrisonhouse.com** for quantity discounts.

BOOKS BY RICK RENNER

*Digital version available for Kindle, Nook, iBook, and other eBook formats.

Note: For audio and video teaching materials by Rick Renner,
please visit **www.renner.org**

BOOKS IN RUSSIAN

Dream Thieves

Dressed To Kill

The Dynamic Duo

Good News About Your New Life

If You Were God, Would You Choose You?

Insights to Successful Leadership

Isn't It Time for You To Get Over It?

Hell Is a Real Place

How To Test Spiritual Manifestations

A Light in Darkness, Volume One

Living in the Combat Zone

Merchandising the Anointing

Paid in Full

The Point of No Return

Seducing Spirits and Doctrines of Demons

Sparkling Gems From the Greek Daily Devotional

Spiritual Weapons To Defeat the Enemy

Ten Guidelines To Help You Achieve
   Your Long-Awaited Promotion!

365 Days of Power

What the Bible Says About Healing

What the Bible Says About Tithes and Offerings

What the Bible Says About Water Baptism

What To Do if You've Had a Failure

The Harrison House Vision

Proclaiming the truth and the power

Of the Gospel of Jesus Christ

With excellence;

Challenging Christians to

Live victoriously,

Grow spiritually,

Know God intimately.